How to Stop Racing through Life
and Start Enjoying the Ride

THE  TRICYCLE WAY

How to Stop Racing through Life
and Start Enjoying the Ride

THE
TRICYCLE
WAY

SANJOG AUL

CTN
PUBLISHING
ROMEOVILLE, IL

CTN Publishing
1235 Windham Pkwy
Romeoville, Illinois, USA 60446

Editing: Marcia Abramson and David Colin Carr
Book Cover Design: Alexander Vulchev
Book Interior Design: David Moratto
Illustrations: Dede Setiawan
Audiobook Narration: Craig Levin

LCCN: 2018904014
ISBN 978-0-9973876-0-5 (Hardback)
ISBN 978-0-9973876-1-2 (Paperback)
ISBN 978-0-9973876-2-9 (Kindle)
ISBN 978-0-9973876-4-3 (EPUB)
ISBN 978-0-9973876-3-6 (Audible)

CONTENTS

Everything in the Universe is within you.
Ask all from yourself.

—Sufi Rumi

A NOTE FROM THE AUTHOR

THE PHONE ON the nightstand read 3:40 a.m., five minutes before the daily alarm was set to go off. Only one email had come in since I'd last checked. Was that half an hour ago, an hour? Wednesday had barely started, and I'd already clocked close to 40 hours at work.

For weeks I'd been trying to stay on top of things. But as I handled one crisis, another flared. With offices in the United States and half a world away in India, I could be working 24 hours a day—and often did. The endless sense of urgency took a toll on all areas of my life. My mind always racing, I never sank into deep sleep. It clouded my decision-making, and my constant stress was ruining our family life. The previous night I'd had a long argument with my wife. One of many—with a well-worn script.

"You're never there for the family, Sanjog.

"You work and work, and have no time for your family. Here I am—raising our children, keeping a home, and helping you in your business. All in hopes that it'll free up time for you to spend with us. But it's only freed up more time for you to work!"

Let me say clearly: my wife is the perfect life partner. But work was my priority. I didn't yet appreciate her role as I flew around the world three months of the year. And when I was home, I worked even harder to catch up on the business backlog.

I learned of many precious moments only through someone else's recollection. My son's and daughter's first steps. Their first words. Many wedding anniversaries. Looking back, I can see I was lucky to still be married.

But my goal was clear, and it was huge. If I worked hard enough, brought in enough money, my family would be happy. All they had to do was just be patient.

"Look at the drawing your daughter made at school to-day," my wife said as I walked in the door from a four-week business trip. It was a crayon sketch of our family — my son, my wife, and my daughter.

"Wait, where am I in this picture?"

My wife stared at me. Any other response would have been redundant. The problem was evident. But the solution wasn't. I was carrying out my duties as the provider. I was ready to sacrifice everything for a paycheck to make my family happy.

"Who are you doing all this for?" she asked.

"Huh?" My mind was already wondering when my staff in India would call.

"Why do you work all the time? For what?"

"What do you think it takes to develop a booming business and the life we want? We have to pay the price if we want all this!" I was looking up at the clock in the family room. The team would call any minute to discuss the status of a critical project. Couldn't she see I needed space to achieve my —I mean our—dreams?

"Why can't you support me?" I snapped. I was exhausted by the trip and frustrated with the nagging. "Why can't you explain to the kids that I'm working hard to provide a better life for them? All this is for them. Because I love them."

"Did you ever think about what they want?"

"What do they want?"

"You, Sanjog. Only you."

In fact, my business wasn't working out the way I'd planned. But my ego wasn't allowing me to quit. I kept pouring in more hours to grow the company—eating into precious family time. I schmoozed every day from early morning until midnight. If my calendar wasn't full of appointments, I felt guilty of being lazy.

My contacts and clients had moved in to fill the emotional void in my life. I was inattentive — not to colleagues, only to my family. When I was in town, I snapped at everyone at home who distracted me from work. An emotionless zombie, I was becoming worse by the day and spiraling out of control.

I booked family vacations at fun places and exotic resorts. But I was either busy working in the hotel room or glued to the phone. My seven-year-old son became cold as if he didn't know me. My daughter, still a toddler, became a little boss, demanding my attention, pushing hard to make me play with her. But with me not around much, she built an excluding world with her mom, brother, and friends at her daycare. I was locked out.

My wife started to revolt, but I wasn't listening. I was busy defending the position that I needed to work hard for the family. The family was unhappy, and I was miserable. My conclusion: I wasn't working hard enough.

One evening I was on the phone with a client while my wife and children stared at their empty plates for twenty minutes, waiting for my attention to begin our dinner. My wife sprang on me the moment I hung up.

"Sanjog! Starting now, when you come into the house you must turn off your phone."

"But..."

"No buts, Sanjog. That's the rule. You need to be with the family. That can't happen if your phone stays glued to your ear."

"OK, OK. I'll do it."

But the very next day I walked into the house, busy on a conference call. Still talking, I went out to the garage to get a file from my car. When I returned, the door was locked.

"Hello! I'm out here!"

Nothing.

"Hello! Can someone open the door?"

Still nothing. I banged the door. Then a baby voice from inside said, "No."

"Hey, kiddo, please open the door."

"Mama said no phone in the house."

"Open the door please." I was getting angry.

"No." The little voice was bolder.

"Please get your mother."

Silence except for little feet running away from the door on the other side.

"Sanjog, I warned you yesterday—no phone in the house! You can stay out in the garage and finish your calls."

I had stopped listening to everyone. My parents, in-laws, and siblings were concerned. They kept telling me to spend quality time with the family, and to take care of my health. But, I continued working nonstop. I even preached to them to follow my model if they wanted to be successful in life.

THE PRICE OF SUCCESS

No matter what you do for a living, I'm sure you like success. You think it must feel great to have an expensive car, a huge mansion, a carefree lifestyle. But is this wealth worth sacrificing everything else in life?

Those ads for luxury cruises and exotic resorts with happy, well-off people looking radiant and loved are merely images—images portrayed by actors and models, not real families. When you start chasing such fantasies, you're riding through life on a big unicycle propelled by only one big wheel—Success.

Running after what you don't have—and fearing you'll lose what you do have—shifts focus away from what you need. The trap is aiming for higher paying jobs, pushing harder to grow your business, and working longer hours.

This chase does pay off with money to spend on expensive houses, cars, gadgets, and vacations. And invitations to the inner circles of movers and shakers, or being guest of honor at social functions. Swiping your credit card feeds your hunger. The hunger is endless, and the hidden invoice is a crazy schedule.

Watch kids and seniors—both want joy and fulfillment. A child's mind and heart are uncluttered and pure. Seniors have learned what's truly important. Some folks in the years between wear blinders in the race for money and fame.

It's OK to work hard for money and fame. But should the journey be so painful that the fruits of your labor taste bitter and make your soul sick?

THE JOURNEY TO DISCOVERY

I had migrated to the USA from India in 1995, as a software programmer, with two suitcases and $300 in my pocket. Over time I built a media company, CIO Talk Network, which continues to be a trusted resource for information technology (IT) leaders in more than 110 countries, with well-known brands as sponsors. I started and grew AVVAL, an IT consulting firm which now has clients across the United States. I also became a professional moderator of C-suite discussions globally. Besides coaching and consulting with IT leaders, professionals, and entrepreneurs, I offered career skills workshops for college students to prepare them for the real world of IT.

I looked like a winner.

But in my own eyes, I was losing. My wife was not beside me, my kids avoided spending time with me, and my friends were elsewhere. I was madly speeding through life alone. And I had developed a life-threatening heart condition that I didn't notice until I looked around when it was almost too late.

I saw two options. To continue rushing toward losing everything, even my life. Or to slow down and observe what was going on within me, assess the gifts I already had, and use them to rebuild a life I wanted.

It wasn't a real choice. And it required a long experimental journey, one filled with hits and misses and rattling experiences.

Along the way, my training as an IT professional kicked in. To me, it was like a systems challenge. I had to deconstruct the problem, find the reasons that were causing the issues, and then figure out how to bring things back on track.

I needed to fix my unicycle. I needed to add satisfaction and smiles as the two rear wheels to create a balance which would bring stability and harmony. I needed to reassemble my life like a tricycle for a smooth ride.

The tricycle reminded me of my childhood. Of innocent times and freedom of when and where I wanted to go in my little world.

A tricycle would slow me down — but for the better. I didn't need to race to feel joy and fulfillment. It would allow me to experience life in a whole new way — with the people I love riding right along with me. And, I could go after success at a reasonable pace while I enjoyed the ride.

Once I realized that I could fix my life by reassembling it like a tricycle, I was a child again, grinning from ear to ear.

I created a model that turned my life around before it was too late. I call it *The Tricycle Way*. It maps life on a tricycle, each part signifying a core attribute, attitude, or action. The model explains how the parts depend on each other for a smooth ride through your life.

I discovered that using this thinking method, you can work your way to success without sacrificing joy and fulfillment. And you can enjoy the fruits of your labor every day, not at some vague future date. Each day you can wake up refreshed, focused, and filled with passion. The result isn't the life you always imagined — it's the life you never dreamed possible.

Are you looking for a way to get off that big hamster wheel? Does turning your life around sound appealing? Come with me as I share my journey of transformation into a life with daily satisfaction, more smiles, and a broader, greater, sweeter-tasting success.

The method is easy. The results are tremendous. The application is instant. All you need is the willingness and courage to change your life for the better.

MY LIFE NOW

When I wake up in the morning, my head is buzzing with freshness and excitement. My eyes open to a life of hope that's bright and full of opportunities. I lie in bed feeling grateful for last night's peaceful sleep and what I have built for myself and my family.

Beside me is my life partner—who cares for me more than I care for myself. She fights with me and sends me to the doghouse, but it's to straighten me out. I check on my sleeping children—healthy bundles of joy who are developing into responsible young adults. I feel blessed to have a close-knit family that offers emotional support and security.

I see myself in the mirror and smile, counting my blessings. I have a business of my own, earn a good living, and have the flexibility to work anytime and from anywhere — and can choose projects that use my natural talent. Even when I travel, I can control my schedule, so it doesn't rob my family of my presence and contribution when needed. I provide for them and grow my business while enjoying the daily ride. What more can I ask?

As I start my morning, instead of checking email on my phone, I pick a book from the bathroom collection and read a few pages to start my day learning about the world around me and how other people see it. It inspires me to explore ways to improve myself and increase my value to others.

My wife and I start the day together. We have tea, catch up on the news, look at the day's schedule, and see if there are ways we can support each other. We try to balance and make the most of our day ahead.

Depending on the weather, I get on my elliptical or walk for 45 minutes. Exercise is on my schedule seven days a week, and it's a lifestyle rather than a chore. It keeps my heart healthy and draws physical and mental energy for the day ahead.

Mostly I turn off the phone, listen to silence, and clear my mind. It allows me to get into a zone, a timeless space. Sometimes I listen to podcasts and audiobooks. During exercise, I may take a call with my team to plan for the day and brainstorm ideas. Before I know it, I'm sweating on the outside and bursting with energy and inspiration on the inside.

After a shower and a healthy breakfast, I make a to-do list

which always includes items to help with the home front, friends, and personal development. I rank them by importance and set a goal to complete at least the top three.

Every day is different. Surprises and challenges are part of the journey and keep it exciting. I take a break every hour, checking off what I've completed and seeing whether I'm still focused on where I'm heading. Dancing or clapping to music refills me with positive energy for the next working hour.

Throughout the day I make a conscious effort to feel good about working on each task. Keeping a smile on my face prevents stress and improves creative interactions with my team, vendors, and customers.

A drop in the energy level or a loss of motivation for the next task indicates that I must stop working. Dragging any longer will steal the smile off my face, and I'll no longer be doing my best. It's time to call it the end of my workday.

I wind down and reconnect with those who matter most —my family. I toss my phone in my end-of-day basket and greet my wife and kids, gladly.

My wife is an excellent cook as well as an entrepreneur

with a long day too. She cooks dinner, and I volunteer to serve it. Our family chats over dinner build strong connections and allow me to do things that involve little thinking—while giving my wife some downtime. We laugh at a social media post, or I challenge the kids with math and word games.

The end of the evening is about looking back at the day, tucking in my daughter, talking to my son about his day, catching up with my wife, and reading a few chapters of a book. With satisfaction in my heart and a smile on my face, I close my eyes and fall into a peaceful deep sleep.

It's my life now. What would yours be?

THE TRICYCLE WAY

My life today is in stark contrast with where it was. It's the life I've chosen and assembled. Now I see achievements as only milestones in the journey. Even as I go after success, the focus is on daily satisfaction and bringing the smiles which make life worth living.

The Tricycle Way has allowed me a life of freedom and fun beyond my dreams. Like alternative medicine, it heals and strengthens from the inside out. My story didn't end on a sad note. I'm still alive, and able to bring joy and fulfillment to my life—while having more success than ever. Now I focus on bringing satisfaction and smiles to others—which draws satisfaction and smiles back to me.

The Tricycle Way is a guide for framing your thoughts. And deeper, a companion for your soul.

In what follows I introduce a few terms as building blocks for assembling a life you can live gladly. Many blogs and books give an in-depth understanding of such terms. But, what I'm offering instead is an easy reference for how they connect to shape who you are and what you feel at any moment.

There are two types of people. Some whine nonstop about life not going well but do nothing about their situation. Others take matters into their own hands. It's never too early or late for whatever you want your life to be, and there's no right time to start working on it.

Since you're already reading this, I trust you are motivated to learn and act, and willing to look within yourself to find answers to make every day count.

Are you looking for a way to end the crazy race and get off the hamster wheel? Or, do you just want to find ways to boost the level of fulfillment, fortune, and fun you're already enjoying? If yes, I've written this book for you. Instead of waiting to learn from your own costly mistakes, learn from mine.

If you choose to go *The Tricycle Way* and rebuild a life

that provides you a healthy balance of daily Satisfaction, more Smiles, and broader, greater, sweeter-tasting Success, that'll be my reward.

THE UNBOXING

Do you remember as a child what it felt like to open a package with your name on it? Imagine now a big box arriving at your house. When you open it you find directions, a tool for assembly, and seven parts:

1. Frame
2. Cushioned Seat
3. Handlebar
4. Pedals
5. First rear wheel
6. Second, rear balancing wheel
7. One big front wheel

Sit down in your favorite chair and start reading the directions: this book. The effort is about changing your thinking, attitude, and behavior. It's about bringing a dramatic shift in your life. I hope that you'll slow down, absorb the thoughts and ideas I'm sharing, and miss no key steps.

Keep this book of directions close to you with a pen attached to it. Review it often to remind you of the parts of your tricycle, your life, and what you must do to maintain it. Dog-ear this book, write in it, mark your favorite passages, and refer to it often. It will help keep your thinking straight and clear.

Now, let's unpack the parts of the tricycle one by one.

CHAPTER 1

THE FRAME

THE FRAME IS the foundation of your tricycle. It is the unified structure that keeps the essential parts connected. If the frame is weak, the tricycle can become weak and unstable. With a sturdy frame, your tricycle can stay intact even with flying rocks and potholes.

Losing your authenticity is like letting
rust eat away at the frame.

———

The Frame represents Authenticity. Losing your authenticity is like letting rust eat away at the frame. It needs a regular checkup for signs of rust or damage. Even the smallest symptom could stem from a much bigger internal issue. Any threat to authenticity needs immediate attention so you can enjoy the tricycle ride without any upsetting breakdowns.

Do you pretend to be rich to fit in with the movers and

shakers? Did you ever inflate your education and experience to get a promotion or a raise? Have you misrepresented your abilities to a prospect? If you did and got away with it, do you keep doing it on a bigger scale? Though you may get ahead, you're weakening your frame.

Fake it till you make it was an expression that caught on as a therapeutic technique to boost the confidence of athletes. It allowed them to experience the feeling of having already reached their goal, which, in turn, motivated them and helped them realize their dream.

But the expression has been misused, leading people to fake their way through life. They adopt it as their ticket to get whatever they want. But the fact is, it's unlikely to further their life or career.

Leading a fake life creates risk and worse—massive amounts of stress. If people find out, it can permanently damage your reputation and even destroy whatever you've built. Stop and consider—is that worth it?

THE IMPORTANCE OF BEING YOU

Authenticity is about being the real you in the way you think, act, and communicate. And doing it without concern for how others see you. It's about being faithful to your inner self. It's about dealing with people and situations in an open and frank manner. And doing it without worrying about conventions, outcomes, or what's at stake. But be careful with your choice of words, because it's about being candid, not caustic.

Let me introduce you to Jim, Sue, and Heather who appear throughout this book in vignettes that illustrate my points. Jim and Sue run a struggling construction business. Their daughter Emily is seven. Heather, a retired CEO, wanted to keep working, but at a slower pace. She met Jim and Sue at her local chamber of commerce and liked them, so she came on board as business manager to help them grow their business. These characters portray a combination of people I know or have coached. At times you may find yourself in them as if they're living your journey.

"Honey, I have a surprise for you. Look outside," Jim's voice rang with excitement.

Sue made her way to the front window, with Emily behind, praying, "Please let it not be a car." Unfortunately, her prayer missed the mark. A red soft-top convertible sat in the driveway.

"It's pretty cool, eh? I negotiated it down to a steal. That salesman didn't know who he was dealing with."

"Are you out of your mind, Jim?" Sue and Jim had agreed that they'd never raise their voices around Emily, but at that moment Sue was having a tough time keeping calm.

"Jim, we talked about this!"

"I know, I know. But my clients expect a certain professional image. I can't pull up to business meetings in a minivan. What impression of me would that convey?"

"That you're a family man, not some show-off."

"That's not fair, honey."

"Why do you need to impress anyone, Jim? We moved from New York to get away from that lifestyle."

"I know what I'm doing. I was the top man in a very successful contracting firm, and one has to do these things to keep an image."

"Have you forgotten what else came with that title? High blood pressure, no time for us to relax together, and many sleepless nights. I said 'yes' to your proposal because you agreed to stop all that nonsense. We decided not to ruin our lives for that image. But the real issue is: can we afford a sports car right now?"

"We can manage it, Sue. Before we had Emily, you were on your way up in your career. I know it's just a matter of time before you'll start working full-time again. Then we wouldn't need to worry about money."

"Jim, it hasn't been for lack of trying. I'm only bringing in a temp salary working at the design agency. And it all goes just to pay for groceries."

"Don't you have faith in me? My company is about to take off. I'm so close — I can taste it. I need to keep up the image, so people feel that they're working with someone who is successful."

"Jim, you're talented. You have nothing more to prove by buying a tiny car that's too small for a car seat."

"We still have the minivan."

"That's not my point. You're working too hard to look like something you think other people want. People want you — Jim Jenkins."

"I wish things were that simple, Sue."

When Jim arrived at work the next day, Heather looked troubled. "Jim, can we talk?"

"Sue called you, didn't she? She doesn't understand — but you do, right? You know I have to maintain the image of a successful businessman."

"You're wrong, Jim," Heather looked him straight in the eye.

"Come on, Heather! You worked for a big company. I'm sure they expected you to wear expensive suits, drive a luxury car, and live in an upscale neighborhood, right?"

"I avoided playing that game because that's all it is — a game. I was successful by being who I was, not trying to impress people. I was always frank, honest, and genuine."

"Here's my issue, Heather. I don't want people to discover that I'm having trouble even paying my bills. Otherwise, why would they trust doing business with me? Wouldn't you want to work with only successful and stable vendors?"

"Jim, they want to work with the real you. The one who has the skill and is willing to work hard and delivers what he promises. That's what builds trust."

"Have we heard from All Corporation?" Jim changed the subject, as he wasn't winning the argument with Heather.

"Yes, we did."

"Great! When do we start?"

"We don't," said Heather.

"I can't believe this. I had such a great meeting with all the key people. What happened?"

"I talked to Shirley, the facilities director. I hate to tell you—the meeting with you changed their decision. It seems you kept bragging about all the great things you've done, the exotic vacations and cars. It was all about you. They want a person who is real and sincere. Someone they can trust."

Jim didn't know what to say.

"Listen, Jim—I've also been looking at our company books. You've been overspending. Fancy dinners. Gifts. We can't afford it. Especially when you're not bringing in new business. What you're doing is not sustainable. It's time to rethink how you'll keep the lights on and grow your business."

Jim realized that all the money he was spending to impress people wasn't getting him where he wanted to go. It wasn't converting people into clients. He wasn't honest with anyone—including himself. That was hurting both his family and business.

He couldn't fix everything overnight, but he had an idea about where to start.

"Hey Sue, look outside," he yelled when he got home that evening.

Her heart sank again. She had seen the bank and loan statements that afternoon. They had no savings, massive loans, and bills were piling up.

"Are you serious, Jim? Haven't you learned your lesson? We're in trouble here." Sue was busy handling Emily and not sure what Jim was up to again.

"Come on, look outside."

Sue hoped it wasn't another car. She was wrong, but this car made her smile.

"But how, how did you...?"

"Simple. I went back to the dealer and exchanged our car back." Jim was relieved to see the smile on Sue's face. It was the car he'd had for the last eight years, which still drove like a champ.

"You were right, honey. You're right most of the time. Don't let that go to your head though." Jim chuckled. "But I've learned my lesson. I'm going to try to be me and stop trying to impress people. It hasn't worked, and it's only left me stressed."

"Welcome back, Jim. How about taking Emily and me for a drive, and picking up ice cream along the way?"

It's critical to know who you are and stay true to it.

———

Authenticity is daring to be yourself no matter how scary, strange, or awkward it feels. It's really liberating. Others may consider you rash, an oddball, or a maverick. But don't play safe trying to be someone you're not. In the long run, in fact, it isn't safe.

THE INAUTHENTICITY TRAP

Can you live your life behind a mask? People do it every day. But it can eat into the strength of your soul and rob you of the satisfaction and smiles you were born to enjoy.

Have you met people who pretended to enjoy your company—until they got what they wanted from you? How did that make you feel? Used, unappreciated, exploited? Once you realize what such people are all about, do you want to stay friends or even associate with them?

You may think: *I want to stay authentic, but there is always something at stake—like a relationship or a business opportunity. What do I do then?*

> **Inauthenticity is a drug. The more you use, the more you'll crave, and it can destroy you.**

There will always be temptations. Lying, twisting reality, or sugarcoating words seems easy to do. If you end up getting what you want by faking, you'll do it again since losing authenticity looks like a small price to pay. But with time, inauthenticity, like a drug, becomes an addiction. The more you use it, the more you'll crave it. It can destroy you.

When I started my business, I was anxious to make it work at any cost. An opportunity came to bid on a software development contract. I submitted my proposal with inflated credentials. To win the deal, I promised an unreasonably short timeframe for completion and a throwaway price. To my peril, I got the contract—which had massive penalty clauses for project delays.

With a limited budget, I couldn't afford expert software developers. I built a team of contractors with average skills, but even those consultants demanded unusually higher rates because of the time crunch. My clock was ticking—I had no choice. The team was in three different time zones, and I hadn't quit my day job to keep on top of them.

The contractors turned out to be unreliable and some of them left abruptly in the middle of the project. I had to roll up my sleeves and learn new technical skills to finish the project with whatever help I had. And what we produced wasn't acceptable to the client, who rightfully refused to pay the remaining balance. But, I still had to pay the subcontractors. After months of 20-hour days, I ended up losing face and over $34,000. So much for being inauthentic.

STAYING AUTHENTIC ALWAYS

Have you faced a setback in your job or business because you lied or twisted facts? It's a lesson learned the hard way. Inauthenticity may promise short-term gains, but you could end up paying a steep price, as I did. Accept the reality, clean up your act, and promise yourself to stay authentic moving forward.

Don't care about what others think and how
they measure you based on their scale.

Did you face hardship due to circumstances beyond your control — a layoff or a canceled contract due to a budget freeze? When you are in financial trouble, survival instincts kick in which can push you to the extreme and put your character to the test.

Remember: it's still only a test. Stay authentic and focus on your values. Be patient and have reasonable expectations of yourself. Don't care about what others think and how they measure you based on their scale. Face the difficulties by using your gifts. Pay attention to solving the problem at hand. Authenticity will offer you strength and wisdom — the elements you need to bounce back.

Have you ever partnered with others in some wrongdoing where your honesty now could damage their success, and even yours? Did you do it because you wanted to fit in with the group or were looking to gain from it? Should you restore your authenticity if it puts others in harm's way?

You can. And you should. The longer you wait, the worse it gets. Your only choice is to take control. Don't dance around the situation to avoid offending others. Gather your courage and speak up. While you may still pay some penalty for your wrongdoing, you'll prevent a total breakdown of your tricycle.

A few years into my business, my firm contracted with a large company. They were using our offshore software development capability. Nearing completion of one of the projects, we scheduled a conference call with the client.

My partner and I jumped on the call a few minutes early. While we were waiting, my partner mentioned that a particular software component needed redesign since it wasn't working as expected. Though we could fix the issue and still keep the delivery date, the changes would mean more cost for us because of the fixed price contract. We could have ignored the issue and the client would not have known. I told her we needed to stay authentic, keep the client informed, take ownership, and fix it at our expense. I instructed her to stick to the highest quality standards, whatever it took.

You are what you do when you have nothing,
and when you have everything.

———

"That's what I wanted to hear, Sanjog," the client said. "I joined the call first and heard your whole conversation. Thank you for being a real partner."

After that, conversations with this client changed. They kept asking us to do more work and approved our proposals without hesitation. They knew we'd do the right thing even when no one was watching.

You are what you do when you have nothing, and when you have everything. Authenticity, as your guide in all situations, forms a solid foundation for your tricycle.

CHAPTER 2

THE CUSHIONED SEAT

WITH YOUR FRAME established, take out the cushioned seat from the tricycle box. It represents Gratitude.

Be thankful for whatever gifts life offers. Count your blessings and take nothing for granted. Celebrate what you have, without pride. It can be gratitude for providing a safe and modest living for your family. Or, for the friends who share your journey of life. Or, even for your ability to see, hear, speak, walk, and touch.

> *With gratitude, you see setbacks as setups for more favorable outcomes.*

When you ride over life's bumps and potholes, gratitude helps absorb the jarring shocks. With gratitude, you see setbacks as setups for more favorable outcomes. You look at life as a set of lessons and feel thankful even for the tests which help you grow.

Keep expanding your list of blessings. When you're thankful for whatever you have in life, you don't complain about what's missing or not right. The more gratitude you feel, the more cushioned and comfortable the seat becomes.

As I achieved some success, somewhere I lost track of what got me there. I took full credit for whatever good happened to me and criticized the world when things went wrong. I expected others to be at my service, doling out attention, care, and opportunities. I wanted others to do things my way. When they didn't, I pounced on them. A business partner once told me, "Sanjog, our team doesn't want to work on your projects. You don't utter a word of appreciation for all the things they do right. But when they miss the mark, you send long emails criticizing them." In the absence of gratitude, I was a dry soul with a caustic tongue.

Filled with gratitude now, I am a nurtured spirit. I had a massive setback in my business that required laying off most of my employees and starting afresh. My wife, my son, my daughter—within a few horrific years, each of them nearly lost their life in surgery and accidents. Many other incidents shocked me. But sitting on the cushioned seat of my tricycle, filled with gratitude—I stayed positive, calm, and confident.

A close friend said to me, "Nothing seems to throw you, Sanjog." With a warm smile, I responded, "I have more than many can only imagine. I'm blessed—and that's what gives me strength."

PRACTICING GRATITUDE

Sue left the agency and joined Jim in the business. Her passion was interior design for children, especially for kids who never had a permanent home. The home was core to Sue. Her father had been a doctor in the military, so she never attached to one place as a child. She wanted to make other children's dreams a reality by creating unique rooms for them to play in and have fun.

But the business faced endless challenges, making Sue grumpy, and she constantly complained about nothing going right.

"This work isn't what I expected, Heather," Sue said pouring coffee after a long client call. "I thought I could help Jim and follow my dream as an interior designer. His projects needed my design skills and it seemed like a perfect opportunity. I thought the business would grow more than it did last year, but things aren't going as planned. To be frank, I feel a little lost doing what Jim needs."

Heather patted her back. "You need a break. I'm going to the Two Pines Home in Virginia this weekend. You'll like it there. It's a housing facility for children with special needs who have no family. It's a great place for these kids, with medical support for the more fragile ones. They want me to join their advisory board and have invited me to tour the campus. Why don't you come along? It'll be good for you to get away. My treat."

"Sounds like a good idea. I do need a break. When

do we leave? I'll have to arrange things for Emily and Jim. He has no clue how to handle the home front." They both chuckled.

"Saturday morning. And we'll be back before Sunday evening. I'm sure Jim can handle things for a weekend."

Heather and Sue spent the day touring the facilities and meeting the children. It shook Sue up to see how hard those kids worked to learn even basic daily skills. She was deeply moved to see the staff shower love on them — even more than they would have received from their birth parents.

It was an emotional trip for Sue. It reminded her of the painful and complicated pregnancy with Emily, of the nightmares of her newborn having severe issues and needing special care. But that little angel turned out to be a bundle of energy and joy.

When Sue returned home, she couldn't wait to tell Jim.

"You have to visit Two Pines. My heart cries for those kids. They may end up waiting their whole life to be part of a family." Sue couldn't stop her tears.

"I looked in the kids' rooms. All of them need a make-over. I want to redo the interior to make each room unique and beautiful so that those kids can dream and be happy. That's the least I can do for them."

She kept talking over dinner. "I'd like to paint murals on the walls and change floor tiles and replace the stodgy furniture. I'll ask the local home improvement stores to donate supplies."

"It's a fantastic idea. I'm sure everyone will step up for such a great cause. Heather can ask the board to seek volunteers to help. Go for it. I'm so proud of you," Jim said, full of respect for what she was willing to do for those special children.

She was all pumped up and ready for action. It felt great having Jim by her side—loving, supporting, and believing in her. Despite occasional arguments, Jim had always been there for her, through thick and thin.

Sue woke up early and started making calls. Within a few days, she arranged for the community to help with the makeover project. The mayor ran a donation drive and then hosted a special ceremony to unveil the redecorated rooms. At the local event, leaders gave speeches, thanking Sue for taking the lead. There was live media coverage—Sue was the star. But Sue's real reward came in the countless hugs from the children who loved their new rooms. Her heart overflowed with gratitude for having the talent and getting the opportunity to make a difference in their precious lives.

Gratitude works like morning sunshine, clearing away the fog of misery. It brings energy, hope, and healing.

———

Gratitude works like morning sunshine, clearing away the fog of misery. It brings energy, hope, and healing. It doesn't change what happens next or lies ahead, but it gives you the strength to rebuild your life and move forward.

Gratitude reminds you to think of what you have, instead of fixating on what you've lost or never had. You see setbacks as opportunities to learn, to grow, and to face challenges with confidence.

When others do good things for you, if you say *thank you* only as a social gesture, it disappoints them. When you're sincere, others appreciate it and feel motivated — and the connection you build is fantastic. You nurture that person's soul — and your own. Besides, you feel blessed for having people in your life who care and are there for you.

> **Start being thankful for people, events,**
> **and things you've taken for granted.**

I took my son and father-in-law to an out-of-state soccer game — usually a two-hour drive. With Friday afternoon traffic and rain, it took us over four hours. We arrived hungry and tired at the hotel and wolfed down the home-cooked dinner my wife had sent along. Then we crashed.

In the morning I called my wife as she was driving to her yoga class. I asked if she'd like to join us and bring my daughter and mother-in-law to surprise my son and father-in-law. At home 150 miles away, she thought I was crazy, but it sounded like fun.

She skipped yoga and drove back to our house. Within the hour she had prepared food for the whole family and was on her way. I asked the hotel manager to give her access to our room.

As my son unlocked the door after the game, everyone

screamed with surprise. The family was together for home-cooked food and a fantastic adventure for the next two days.

Driving back, I was in tears, filled with gratitude for having a loving family and the ability to afford such fun trips together.

Do you remember reaching the office or home before the downpour? Enjoying hot soup for a winter lunch? Making it through traffic lights without having to stop for a red?

To introduce daily gratitude into your life, start being thankful for people, events, and things you've taken for granted. If you support others, be grateful for the resources and abilities you have to do that.

Find ways you can serve and make a difference in other people's lives. Seek out opportunities to help your community. Share your knowledge. These activities will remind you of how much you have.

An hour before I wrote this section, I was playing a board game with my kids. No one was on their phones. It was a half hour of pure joy, laughter, and bonding. Priceless!

Look within and around you—you'll find gratitude in limitless supply in the little things in life. You're blessed more than you realize.

CHAPTER 3

THE HANDLEBAR

TIME TO RETURN to the box for the handlebar, which helps you turn corners, steer around potholes, and stay on the path. It represents Purpose.

Think about what you love to do — what you're willing to spend most of your time doing for the foreseeable future. How about a natural talent that can fulfill other people's needs and earn you a living? You have to be practical, since you may have obligations and duties.

Does a purpose have to be practical? Not always. It can be selfless. But to live it as much as possible, your purpose must bring a spark to your life and help you become the best you can be.

Try riding a tricycle with a twisted handlebar. It won't be fun. You'll move ahead, but it will be awkward, painful, and confusing. It will strain your body because you won't be sitting in alignment. If you loosen your grip on the handlebar, your tricycle may even turn over.

Sometimes as you ride your tricycle, you'll face unknown situations, feel as if you've lost your way in the weeds or got stuck in the mud. How do you get back on track? By using the handlebar: your purpose.

Earlier in her life, Sue's journey didn't align with her purpose. On the surface, she felt she had it all. She only had to follow the exact path laid out for her by her father, a doctor. Her mother was a doctor. Her two sisters were also doctors. When her turn came, she'd be a doctor, too. The schools, internships, and firm she would work for after graduation, were all planned and arranged.

Except for one problem: in her heart, Sue didn't want to be a doctor. She was smart enough, but she had no passion for medicine. It felt like an obligation to follow the path laid out for her. Every day she went to class felt like a self-imposed prison. There were nights she cried in her dorm room so no one would see how lost she was in her life.

By her third year, with no ambition in her heart,

making it to class became harder and harder. Her grades slipped but she had no drive to get them back up. She was at a crossroads—to continue with med school or find a new path. She was afraid to disappoint her family, and she worried that she'd fail and get kicked out.

"What can I do? I don't have it in me anymore," she asked Dr. Linn, her adviser.

"You're an excellent student, Sue. Your test scores placed you in the top percentile. But your grades are falling. What's going on?"

"I just don't have the drive. I wake up every morning and debate whether to continue with the medical degree or quit and move back home. If I quit and don't become a doctor, it will devastate my family."

Dr. Linn thought for a moment, then responded. "I come from a very different background. My family immigrated to this country with no money. My parents wanted a better life for the eight of us, but they had to work on farms most of their lives just to feed and clothe us. They had no idea about how to apply for college. I loved science and wanted to get into a good university. I worked hard and knew in my heart that one day I'd be a doctor."

"How did you know you wanted to be a doctor?" With her tears dry, Sue was leaning in to listen.

"I was inspired by how the doctors saved my grandmother from a deadly infection. I was eight and visited her at the hospital every day. And when her doctor came for rounds, I had endless questions—about medicines, surgery, and recovery. He patiently answered all of them. I knew then that someday I'd become a doctor because I wanted to save people like my granny. It was clear that my purpose in life was to cure others. That one mission drives everything I've done in medical school, as a surgeon, and now as a professor here.

"But my journey wasn't easy. Even with scholarships, I had to work many jobs to pay for school. When I hit a rough patch, felt distracted, or was tempted to quit, I connected with my purpose. It always brought me back to the right path.

"So, Sue, what do you think you want to be? Not what others want you to become—I want to know what you think your calling is."

"I want to create beautiful homes for children," Sue said with no hesitation. "I once mentioned to my family that I wanted to go into interior design. They laughed as if I was joking, so I never brought it up again."

"No one has to live your life except you, Sue." Dr. Linn leaned forward. "I'm not going to tell you what you should do. But if you choose to live your life following your purpose, no matter the challenges, you'll never lose your way. And you'll enjoy the ride."

"Thanks, Dr. Linn. I needed to hear that." Sue clenched her teeth as she envisioned her path ahead.

What are you doing besides paying your bills and bringing food to the table? If nothing much else, you're surviving— not living. It may lead to a life of I wish vs. I am. A bug has an

18-hour lifespan, but you may live for 80 years or even more. Do you want to just drift through your life in a dull asleep-awake cycle? And besides: what are you doing to make this world a better place?

I asked these questions to a senior executive who had lost his cushy corporate job and wanted my guidance. He realized he had coasted without a purpose for a decade and hadn't grown at all.

You can find purpose where your passion, mission, talent, and profession meet.

I was also guilty of leading a purposeless life in the past, and I paid the price for it. My education and experience are in IT. But earlier, with no defined purpose, I used to jump on new business ideas no matter how far removed they were from my interest or expertise. For example, I had a bright idea for a business delivering customized food anywhere in the world, based on a customer's health-taste profile. I spent months chasing chefs, commissaries, doctors, and investors —ignoring my core IT business, and robbing time and focus away from my family.

A philosophy book or professors' theories will not be able to answer questions like: *Why am I here? How should I go about making the most of my existence?* You can't just pop a pill and enlighten yourself. It requires proper attention and self-inquiry to find your life's purpose.

Look where your passion, mission, talent, and profession

meet. There's a need for what you love and are great at doing —and you may get paid for it. Perhaps not right away, but a life aligned with purpose not only brings joy and fulfillment, it's also the best platform for you to earn money and fame.

If you take the time to find your purpose, aligning with it will be simple. Putting it at the center of how, when, where, and what you do to pay bills will make life more pleasant and meaningful. With a defined purpose, you'll have a chance to not only exist but to live a life of meaning that impacts the world.

Knowing your purpose will prepare you for whatever life throws your way. And when it drives you, challenges won't look scary. You'll expect them as part of dreaming, thinking, learning, and preparing your roadmap. In fact, you'll welcome such obstacles because you'll see them as opportunities to learn.

We look up to legends who left a mark on society through their contributions. They found their purpose and aligned their life with it. They had a natural talent which they developed to its full potential, and they used it to create value for others. Their contributions continue to inspire others. As a result, the world honored them with the titles of leadership, and often with money and fame as well.

CHALLENGES IN FINDING PURPOSE

I regularly have conversations with senior professionals who are miserable in their jobs. They drag their feet to work, unable —and in some cases unwilling—to find their purpose.

When you were a child, your parents and relatives told

you where to go and what to do. Those were the *shoulds* to keep you safe and secure. It was their duty, and it was okay at that age. But are you still carrying those *shoulds* as an adult, letting them govern your life, causing you to drift? Many of us do — it's easier to follow someone's instructions than chart a unique path.

Looking inward for answers can be complicated and unnerving. Keeping a safe job and a routine life seems much more comfortable than going after the new and unknown. The fear of uncertainty and the excuse of *I don't know how to find my purpose* can hold you back from trying.

Hardship or temptations may distract you from finding your purpose. But accepting whatever happens as your *destiny* blocks the process of discovering your purpose.

HOW TO FIND YOUR PURPOSE

How do I find my purpose? Have others figured it out? What if it changes over time? You must ask yourself these questions even if they rattle you.

Purpose is not about becoming a billionaire or building the tallest tower.

Ask your parents, relatives, and friends for input, since they know you well — and they saw your gifts in the purest form as you were growing up. What do they see as your natural talent and abilities?

Look inward and ask yourself: *What would you do if you had no fear, no limitations, and you simply couldn't fail? What is it you like to do and lose track of time doing it? What are you willing to do even if no one paid you? Did you visit new places or pick up skills in the last month or year or decade because you wanted to? Do you see any patterns or connections among them?*

Purpose is not about becoming a billionaire or building the tallest tower. What you do for a living may not be the same thing as your calling, but it can still be a way to live your purpose.

**Listen to and trust your inner voice
to help you find your purpose.**

If you are a life coach, purpose could be to help bring real, lasting, and positive change in people's lives. For an attorney, it could be following ethical means to assist people in achieving justice. For a doctor, healing. For a public speaker, motivating the audience to reach their full potential. Get the idea?

You have something unique to offer to this world. To find it, you first need to cut off all the noise, to unwind and take a break. Detach from what you are doing or what is happening to you now. Put aside what others say you should do. Listen to and trust your inner voice to help you find your purpose. While searching, don't be pulled into thinking about how you'll align your life with your purpose once you figure it out. Just explore.

Paint a vision of how life will be with your dreams and

desires fulfilled. What's holding you back? What challenges, fears, limiting beliefs, uncertainties, and doubts? What will make it worth finding your way past these obstacles?

Pour it all out—into words or pictures.

Walk away and come back the next day. Stay focused, and refine your findings. Ask help from a friend or a coach who can serve as a sounding board and give you honest input. You'll see your purpose emerge.

The executive in transition early in this chapter had a keen sense of problem-solving, innovation, and excellent understanding of IT. With some deep thinking on his own, and brainstorming with me and others he trusted, he identified that he'd enjoy bridging the gap between business and IT, especially helping CEOs get better at understanding and adopting IT.

With the clarity of purpose, he dropped the idea of getting another cushy job. He started consulting, and within a year he wrote a book. He now travels internationally—coaching, speaking, and consulting—enjoying every day by living his purpose.

HOW TO ALIGN WITH YOUR PURPOSE

Once you have found your purpose, your inner voice will say, *don't wait any longer. You must live life doing things you were born to do.* But the primary human survival instinct may kick in with questions: *What will my parents, friends, peers, or life partner think? Should I quit my job? Can I live my purpose while keeping my day job? How long will it take to reach a point where I can live my purpose? How will I pay my bills while I make changes to align my life with my purpose?*

Commit to living your purpose while fulfilling your obligations — and stick to it.

The question that tops the list is: *Can I make money and fulfill my obligations while living my purpose?*

Yes, you can.

Look for ways to increase the time you spend living your purpose, both in your day job and your spare time. Or look for a new job with better prospects.

The money will remain a significant factor. How much money is enough to pay your bills and still save for a rainy day? You shouldn't expect or plan a life of luxury, at least in the beginning when you're still working on aligning your life with your purpose.

Commit to living your purpose while fulfilling your obligations — and stick to it. It may be a long journey of transformation, but it will be fun. And you'll find better opportunities to earn more money than you imagined while living a fuller life.

All my business and professional efforts now align with my purpose. My media company and consulting firm have IT focus. I coach IT leaders. I moderate IT management and leadership sessions globally and speak on related topics. If anything else gets my ear, I bow out, referring to people in my network who may be a better fit.

CHAPTER 4

THE PEDALS

NEXT OUT OF the box come the Pedals which represent Giving. Whenever you can, use your talent and resources voluntarily to help others. In business, this means doing more than what you're paid for. In personal and community life, it means giving help with no expectation of anything in return.

With the conscious effort to give, something profound happens. You exceed the expectations of everyone you serve. They are so delighted that they shower you with an appreciation which motivates you to pedal faster and give even more.

You receive less when you only focus on getting.

Do you only offer to help others when you expect them to return the favor? How do you feel when you realize someone is doing that to you? Does wearing your go-getter badge fill you with pride? Or do you think giving is for *nice* people, and that others take advantage of them? You *receive* less when your focus is only on *getting*.

Since childhood, I have been a giver—right through my first few years in business. My inclination for giving resulted in introductions and referrals that led to my first few clients. But gradually, I started shying away from giving, falling for advice from more *worldly* business contacts. I only connected with individuals who were a business prospect or might refer me to a few others. Even with active clients, I started allocating my time based on whether they would bring me more business. Everything and everyone became a means to an end.

This self-centered approach started hurting my credibility within my professional network. Customers, who used to call because I had always been there for them, started avoiding me. Soon I was chasing them like just another sales guy, even to get a meeting. For many, I demoted myself from being a partner to a vendor, from a friend to a parasite. There are a few who still hold that impression of me even after my transformation. The more I aimed at gaining, the more I lost. It has done permanent damage, and I regret it deeply.

When you give, it builds a vast network of people who like you and want to see you succeed.

Giving opens many more doors than only *taking* from others. Giving helps develop connections that aren't based solely on transactions. It allows bonding at a deeper emotional level. It also enables you to develop a greater sense of self-worth as you realize you can offer what others don't have.

When you give, it builds a vast network of people who like you and want to see you succeed. They become a steady source of introductions and referrals, which helps you grow as a person and as a professional, creating opportunities for you to earn more. Such is the power of giving.

Sue watched Jim stuffing his pocket with business cards on the way out the door. Heather was waiting in her car to take them to a Two Pines Home charity fashion show.

"Leave your cards at home, Jim. You won't be making any sales at this event. For once, take a break and enjoy."

To Jim, meeting people was always a fishing expedition. He pitched everyone — at kids' birthday parties as well as church on Sundays. He had fallen into the habit of desperately looking to generate new business. Emily was in elementary school, and Sue was trying to rebuild her career. With more money going out than coming in, he was under a lot of pressure, but none of his gimmicks were working.

"OK, OK, I won't." He didn't want any drama that would carry out to the car in front of Heather.

To his surprise, Jim felt relaxed at the event — meeting new people, not thinking about sales, and having a few laughs. At the cocktail reception, Heather approached him. Walking along with her was a tall, skinny, middle-aged man in an expensive black suit.

"Jim, this is Marty," Heather said. "He's the head of Continental Industries and a trustee on the Two Pines Home board."

"Nice to meet you, Jim."

"Hello, Marty. Nice to meet you."

"Heather tells me you're a building contractor. Do you also work on commercial buildouts?" Marty asked after some small talk.

"Yes, we do," Jim said, hiding his excitement.

"I've done my job introducing you both. I'll let you boys connect and talk shop." Heather smiled and walked away.

"Drink?" Marty asked. They walked to the bar and ordered. While waiting, Marty started telling Jim about his business.

"We're looking to expand our operations and already have a construction site picked out—but we're facing some major issues." Marty's suppliers were unpredictable and were sending poor quality building material. The general contractor failed to manage the project well, so it was already delayed and over budget. The company was scheduled to open a second facility in the next eighteen months—but was having trouble getting the first one operational.

Jim listened, asked questions, and made mental notes. He had handled many situations like this before. Based on the details Marty shared, Jim offered a few tips on how to bring the project back on track. He also offered tips on how to deal with material suppliers and referred a few that he used. For those few minutes, he forgot about getting Marty as a client and only wanted to solve his problems.

"Thanks, Jim. It was great chatting with you. I'll share all this with my team."

"My pleasure, Marty." They shook hands and walked back to the reception area. Jim felt great being able to help.

After the event, while Heather, Jim, and Sue were waiting for the valet to bring her car, Heather patted Jim's back and said, "I don't know what you discussed back there at the bar with Marty, but he seemed impressed. Great job!"

"Yeah, Marty seems like a great guy. He's having some issues with a plant buildout. I gave him a few tips. Nothing big."

"Good. Marty thought you were awesome. He is a great guy to know," Heather said as they all got into her car.

Jim didn't think much about the event. The following week he got a call from Marty.

"Hey Jim, I wanted to reach out and thank you again for your suggestions at the charity function. We followed your recommendations about material suppliers. We're replacing them with the ones you suggested. We also changed things on the project plan. You were spot-on. It should help bring us back on track. The current contractor should've figured it out, but he didn't, so we are going to replace him too. Would you like to come on board and help us finish this expansion? Then help with the second one as well? Can you make a trip to the Continental office and meet the team next week? If that works for you, I'll ask them to send you details, so we have a productive meeting."

"Sure, I'd be glad to help. And yes, next week works for me." Jim tried to hide his excitement.

"Great, see you then. Bye for now." Jim was shaking, still holding the phone in his hand. He couldn't believe someone could trust him based on a five-minute conversation to award such a big contract.

Jim figured out where he'd been going wrong. He was focusing on selling hard to get business. He hadn't realized that people love to buy, but hate to be sold.

He thought about his subcontractors and suppliers. He chose them because they took the time to understand his business and cared about his needs. They had all earned his trust by first helping him solve his problems without looking for anything in return. Just as he did with Marty.

THE ROAD TO BECOMING A GIVER

Giving isn't a sign of weakness. And it's not only for the wealthy and famous. It isn't just about donating money to a charity. Helping your neighbor jump-start a car or supporting a co-worker struggling with a task also counts.

We're all born with a giving gene,
and we can never give enough.

You can give by providing your knowledge, time, and energy. Help your friends, relatives, and people in your personal and professional network with the intent of giving—expecting nothing in return. Work at a soup kitchen. Help out at your place of worship or volunteer at a non-profit whose work you admire. Mentor a classmate or colleague. Make professional introductions while helping an entrepreneur with advice for a startup. Review someone's book and offer candid feedback. Even with paying customers, go the extra mile and deliver beyond what's on the contract. Look around, and you'll see infinite ways to give.

Keep giving—in good and in bad times.

We're all born with a giving gene, and we can never give enough. Embrace giving as a way of life. Don't limit yourself by giving only to those you like or when you feel obliged to return a favor. Give to everyone, and offer yourself as a resource to all. However, first be sure that you're fulfilling your duties and providing for the family.

Some people won't return the favor. That's OK—giving isn't about keeping score. If they need help again, don't hold back.

A customer may not recognize or appreciate you for your extra effort. But keep serving and adding value beyond expectations.

And don't expect your tricycle to go very far by just pedaling once. Keep giving—in good and in bad times. Continue to pedal forward, keeping up the momentum.

GIVING DURING A CRISIS

During a crisis, survival instincts kick in, and your focus turns to bringing back stability. It's draining and may lower your confidence and sense of self-worth. Explore what happens when you embrace giving. When those you support thank you, you'll appreciate what you have. It'll help bring back your confidence and strengthen your emotional resilience in handling stress and hardship.

When you give to others, magic happens.

Losing a loved one can be crushing and may turn the course of your life. Devote yourself to helping others dealing with loss. Giving to others heals your soul and brings your own life back to normal.

RECEIVING IS AS IMPORTANT AS GIVING

When you give to others, magic happens. You'll reap their support and the opportunities they create for you—spreading the word about you and building your fan base in the world. Though they may not always directly return the favor, your act of giving turns them into givers. This way not only those you helped, but the whole universe aligns to support your success and well-being—and creates more givers.

Giving without expecting anything in return doesn't mean you should reject what you receive—from the individuals you helped or from the universe—as a result of your kind deeds. Be open and ready to receive. When you receive with a free heart, it's a return gift to the person giving to you.

A global IT sales leader who I know very well lost his job. I spent many hours with him discussing how to rethink career options and sharing contacts who could help him. No expectations, just helping out a person in need. He joined another large company and without me asking, he recommended my IT media company to his new employer. Before long I was on a conference call with their global marketing leader, discussing specifics of a significant project.

Another time I connected with a senior professional while my team was recruiting him for an IT role. He asked if I could coach his friend who'd been out of work for a year. I not only agreed to help, but did so free of charge. When the professional later landed a top executive position, he invited my consulting firm to help with a few key hires and projects.

Giving is the only way I know now—I'm a firm believer. I keep giving and receive more than most people.

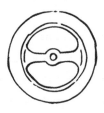

CHAPTER 5

THE FIRST REAR WHEEL

YOU NOW HAVE a sense of how the Frame (Authenticity), Cushioned Seat (Gratitude), Handlebar (Purpose), and Pedals (Giving) connect to your tricycle. It's almost time to get on your tricycle and go, but you need wheels to do that. The first of the two rear supporting wheels is Satisfaction.

When you meet achievement targets you've set for yourself—like a strong effort toward an outcome, or providing well for your dependents—you experience satisfaction. And when others deliver as promised, meeting or exceeding your expectations, it leads to satisfaction.

WHERE DO YOU GO WRONG?

Living under unreasonable expectations of yourself—perhaps a sense of urgency that makes you feel like you're in a race, or taking on a herculean task for which you aren't ready—you miss finding satisfaction.

If someone, where you work, has a title or salary you want, work toward earning it. But don't set a crushing deadline to accomplish it. Setting unreasonable expectations creates pressure and tempts you to skip some thinking and planning steps required to do things right. When you don't see the result —ouch! Major disappointment, and dissatisfaction.

> **Don't worship what you lack.**
> **It robs you of daily satisfaction.**

Don't try living up to the standards you feel others have created for you. Checking off items on your long to-do list may get you occasional moments of delight. But it robs you of daily satisfaction.

Looking in the opposite direction, are your expectations of others realistic? Do you recognize their challenges and limitations? Do you expect them to drop everything and attend to you first? And when there are delays due to circumstances beyond anyone's control, do you look for someone to blame or go ballistic? These reactions deprive you of satisfaction.

Don't go to sleep counting tasks you couldn't complete today or are due tomorrow. Don't wake up thinking there isn't enough time for so much you have to do. Don't worship what you lack—that, primarily, robs you of daily satisfaction.

Success gives a temporary high that can be addictive. When you don't reach it, or there is a broad gap between the two highs, it seems like a failure—which pulls you down.

When you focus on daily satisfaction, you'll remain stable between the peaks of success.

Putting satisfaction over success may seem like laziness. But when you focus on satisfaction first, you have much more mental, physical, and emotional energy for working toward your goals—which keeps the journey pleasant all the way.

HOW TO FIND SATISFACTION?

You can enjoy daily satisfaction even in the imperfect and demanding life we live today. The core parts of the tricycle— Authenticity, Gratitude, Purpose, and Giving—are the keys to satisfaction.

STAY AUTHENTIC TO STAY SATISFIED

Be your true self in the way you think, speak, and act. Don't wear a mask. Staying authentic helps you to set realistic expectations—for yourself and others—that can be met. It paves the road to ongoing satisfaction.

A singer started her journey by creating music that satisfied her. She wrote all her own lyrics and bared her soul in the songs—expressing her real thoughts, moods, and feelings. People loved her music—which brought her fans, fame, and fortune, and made her a star.

But then the evils of stardom caught up with her. Pressured by record labels and tour promoters, she changed her focus to staying top of the charts. She stopped creating music she and her fans loved. To her surprise, the new songs tanked on the charts, and her concerts no longer sold out. She lost many fans, and those who stayed demanded that she sing only her old songs.

She realized that moving away from her authentic core was hurting her. She took charge, creating music again as she used to, expressing her real self. Her songs climbed to the top of the charts, and she regained her fans. Plus, her satisfaction returned, along with all that she'd lost.

LET GRATITUDE LEAD TO SATISFACTION

Take a few moments to think about what you don't have. Recollect situations that didn't work out for you. Include people who didn't treat you well or betrayed your trust. It might be a long list. As you consider the list, how do you feel? Disappointed and hopeless? You may feel drained and lose interest in anything new or exciting. Looking at a glass half empty exhausts a soul and makes the journey more difficult.

Now count what you have. Do you have loved ones who are safe and healthy? Do you earn enough to feed the family and spend time with them? Do you get to break away from the routine and share laughter and stories with your friends? If yes, you have more than many others. Practicing gratitude is key to satisfaction.

LEAD A LIFE OF PURPOSE AND GIVE MORE FOR SATISFACTION

When you're paying bills, saving for the future, and working hard for money and fame—lead with purpose. When you know where you're heading, it focuses your efforts. When you stay true to your purpose, satisfaction follows.

When you're working on any task for yourself or others, be a giver putting in your absolute best. With sincere effort, you'll hold yourself high in your own eyes. Ahh, that's satisfaction.

In testing times, engage in giving. Help others ease their pain. Giving helps you realize that you're not the only one suffering hardships and that problems can be solved. If you can help others with their issues—you can fix your own. The feelings of hope and positivity that arise lead to satisfaction.

THE TWO SPOKES OF SATISFACTION WHEEL

Accepting situations beyond your control, and making steady progress, ensure daily satisfaction.

Though Sue had found her purpose and started her journey toward flourishing as an interior designer, the road felt bumpy. She whined and complained. When things didn't meet her expectation, she turned angry and depressed—which was evident in her dealings with customers, vendors, and friends.

Though to her, life was crashing down, no one else could see a problem. Her life was comfortable, Emily was healthy, and their home was beautiful. Though she was living her purpose, it wasn't enough. She felt anxious and miserable. She whined that her client list wasn't as long as her competitors' who had been in business much longer. She compared her four-bedroom house to bigger homes she saw driving around the city.

Her attitude started impacting the family as well. She was snapping at Emily and telling Jim how nothing would work out. She threatened to drop it all and go back to being a homemaker—or leave everyone and walk out of their lives. Jim and Emily loved her but didn't know how to help her.

"I still don't have enough clients, and it's been almost two years since I started."

"Why can't any of these vendors do their job right? It's crazy. I should fire them all."

"These customers are such a pain. They want all my time, the best service, but don't want to pay enough to get me out of bed in the morning."

It wasn't the first time Heather heard Sue yelling. Anyone could listen to her rant from the other end of the office—and way too frequently. Heather was concerned, and Jim had asked her in confidence to see if she could help Sue since nothing he tried was working.

Something had to change—but it wasn't the outside world. Heather knew she had to help Sue shift how she viewed herself, the people she was dealing with, and the world overall.

"Sue, let's call it a day. Let's have lunch out and let's make another field trip."

"Heather, it's only 11 a.m. on a Tuesday. Sorry, but I can't." Sue looked at Heather for a second and then resumed shuffling papers on her desk. "I've got so much to do. I need more clients, or else my business won't survive. I'd love to take the day off—trust me, I want to. But I've got way too much going on."

"Is something on fire, Sue?" Heather asked, lifting her chin in a way that signaled she meant business.

"What do you mean?"

"Is something on fire, Sue? Do you have a meeting today? Or is a proposal due?"

"Not until Thursday."

"Then let's go. I heard you scream a few moments ago. And this is not the first time. I know you're feeling stuck and frustrated. But how you're handling it is not helping you, your business, and others around you. If you trust me, then pick up your coat and meet me outside. I'll be waiting in the car."

"I don't have a choice in this, do I?" Sue picked up her coat and switched off the lights.

"No." Heather faked a karate stance, and they both laughed.

Laughing felt good. Sue noticed her own bitterness but didn't know what to do. Heather had become a close friend, and she'd come to trust her experience and judgment. So, she agreed to get some fresh air and see if Heather could help her fix things.

They stopped at a local diner for coffee and then drove to the Biltmore, a classic, elegant hotel.

"What are we doing here?" Sue asked as Heather stopped the car at the hotel entrance for the valet.

"Working in a large company as a leader, I had to

keep my thinking fresh and clear. For that, I looked for people with unbiased opinions as a sounding board for ideas. A friend referred me to this mastermind group — successful entrepreneurs who meet every two weeks to discuss their business challenges and help each other. It worked out great for me in the past. I enjoy learning new things, so I've kept my membership active. You're attending as my guest. Trust me, Sue — it'll be worth your time."

Heather had already registered Sue before leaving the office. The receptionist greeted them and escorted them through the lobby to one of the most beautiful ballrooms Sue had ever seen. About twenty people were sitting around an expensive mahogany table. Others were at the lunch buffet, chatting and filling up their plates. It looked more like a country club on a Sunday. Everyone seemed to be having a great time.

"Wow, is this a business meeting?"

"What did you expect?" Heather asked.

"Isn't it supposed to be more intense and formal so they can discuss their challenges and grow their companies?"

"Do you think a successful business is about wearing suits and being intense?"

"All I know is my business is not growing, and I'm having no fun at all."

"That's why I brought you here, so you can learn how to turn things around. You're in for a treat." Heather grinned as she introduced Sue to the group. The informal discussion continued with a mix of ideas, jokes, and members roasting each other. To her surprise, Sue learned quite a bit. She took a lot of notes as people shared their issues and others gave advice on how to solve them.

"So how was it? What did you think of the group?" Heather asked as they were driving back.

"It was incredible. I've never seen a group so charged up about business and life. There wasn't a single soul there who was worked up about their hardships."

"So, what did you learn today?"

"That I'm my worst enemy. Worrying and trying to control everything is what's making me miserable. And I'm making everyone around me unhappy. I've got to learn to accept what I cannot change, and focus on making a little progress every day."

"Well then, mission accomplished!"

Sue had found the keys to satisfaction: Acceptance and Progress.

THE ACCEPTANCE SPOKE OF SATISFACTION WHEEL

Do you expect life to present itself as if you control what's going on? It's OK to hope for an ideal life to keep you motivated, but assuming everything will go according to your plan leads only to dissatisfaction.

Like a boat in a fast-moving river, life carries you along with the current. Acceptance is agreeing to the reality of the river, recognizing that no pushing or pulling will alter its course.

Don't kick yourself for what's happened — or blame others, or allow setbacks to cripple you. Don't drop everything and get all wound up investigating events which neither you nor science can explain.

I'm sure there is a reason for at least some setbacks or hardships. If you can find what went wrong, the learning experience will put your mind to rest. But what if you face a tragedy like losing a loved one? Or have a disabling accident, or get laid off from your job, or face business failure? You can't do anything about those. You can't reverse the clock to undo what's happened. So why put the rest of your life on hold?

Change the changeable if you can
but accept the unchangeable.

Acceptance is neither complacency nor denial. It's the flexibility and willingness to see things as they are and to look beyond. Change the changeable if you can, but accept the unchangeable. It's not easy to accept some situations. But doing it will restore your satisfaction.

I know a great married couple — senior professionals with an impressive income, a fancy lifestyle, and lovely children. A few years ago, one of their kids developed a rare, incurable disease. It shattered them. Unable to accept the reality, for a few years, they drowned in misery and depression, locking themselves at home with no friends, parties, or vacations. It only made things worse for the whole family, especially the affected child.

Only with acceptance of what had happened could they restore their satisfaction and focus on rebuilding the confidence of their afflicted child and living their own life again to the fullest.

GRATITUDE HELPS WITH ACCEPTANCE

Gratitude, a foundational value of *The Tricycle Way*, is the best attitude for accepting life, people, and situations as they are and as they aren't.

I love grapefruit—its unique taste blends sweet and sour. Think of your life as a grapefruit. Its yummy sweetness allows you to accept its sourness. Appreciating life's gifts makes it easier to accept what may be taken away at times.

I know a woman who has a rough ride as the wife of a busy, struggling, and often absent businessman, but gratitude keeps her afloat. Business issues, family challenges, and financial hardships never stop. When it's raining, she lets it rain, thankful for everything she has and riding through her days on satisfaction.

My own experience is parallel. My business was my labor of love. I gave my time and talent to nurture it and see how far I could take it. I expected it to keep growing. But it went up and down like a rollercoaster, which drove me nuts—I was doing everything per my plan and to the best of my abilities. Focusing on what wasn't working in the plan, I was always angry, frustrated, and stressed.

I'd been married for only a few years, and I wanted my wife to think my way, behave as I expected, and change to my liking. I wasn't thankful at all for what she did for me or brought to the marriage. Instead of accepting, I was expecting everything and everyone to dance to my tune. It made my life a painful wrestling match. It was a horror movie with a never-ending climax.

*Acceptance helped me look beyond the setback
and see the pit as a seed.*

Turbulence in my life and business hasn't yet gone away. But by staying thankful for what life has offered me, I'm able to accept others as they are and situations I cannot control.

There came a time when I had to close offices, lay off employees, and start again from scratch. But acceptance helped me look beyond the setback and see the pit as a seed. It allowed me to do a major reset and rethink my business—which led to a much better result.

I still field curveballs that beat me. But armed with gratitude, I accept what is happening, learn from the experience, and stay satisfied.

THE PROGRESS SPOKE OF SATISFACTION WHEEL

The second spoke of the Satisfaction wheel is Progress. Making regular progress toward your goal leads to satisfaction—which further motivates you to keep charging ahead.

Do you have ambitious personal and professional goals that you'd like to achieve tomorrow? It takes time, effort, and multiple orderly steps to build a castle. Inch your way forward with realistic goals. Whether it's your relationship, a business you started, or a project at home, focus on progress.

I've been growing my media company for many years and put in a lot of hard work. But it's the focus on progress that has led my company to become a trusted thought leadership resource for senior IT executives globally. And I'm not done yet.

Think about the website you want to develop or the relationship you want to repair with your partner. It may take much longer than you expected, and the outcome may not be what you envisioned. But is that the end? You have the choice of being frustrated or feeling good that you made progress and got closer to your ideal.

AUTHENTICITY DRIVEN PROGRESS

The core value of authenticity is a crucial factor in making progress. That was evident when I coached an executive who wanted to be an expert in a particular field. When we met, he said he'd do whatever it took to reach that goal. He had a few years of appropriate experience and seemed to know enough to hold a job. But to get to the level he wanted to reach, he had to gain a lot more knowledge and on-the-job experience.

We developed an action plan. The executive showed excitement during the coaching calls and meetings—but didn't make much actual progress. The excuses: not getting enough time, the roadmap needed rethinking, and so on. Something wasn't right.

When we met for the next coaching session, I asked if he had real intentions of becoming an expert in that field. His response was, "No, it doesn't interest me as much, now that I'm trying to dig deeper. I told you that I'm passionate about this, but I was lying. I know other people who are masters in this field, and they make a lot of money. I thought if I could somehow build the image of being an expert, I could do the same."

We discussed how faking passion wasn't getting him anywhere. He realized his mistake and promised to be honest with me moving forward. We went back to the drawing board, discussed his real passion, changed course, and built a new roadmap. He kept his promise. Being true to himself, he's now making significant progress toward his goal.

Stay authentic—you won't kid yourself about your capabilities and what you can achieve in a given timeframe. You won't waste time in acts of make-believe or cover up your failures. You'll know what you should be doing, take responsibility for it, and make real progress.

PURPOSE HELPS WITH PROGRESS

As the handlebar of your tricycle, purpose plays a crucial role in steering progress. You may have many dreams. Follow the one for which you have a credible answer to the question: *Why should I do this?*

In planning each day, put the tasks that align the most with your purpose at the top of your to-do list. You'll feel excited about putting in your best effort to complete those tasks. Even if you finish only the top three, you'll feel great and make significant progress by staying aligned with your purpose.

Let your purpose help drive progress. Instead of meeting deadlines, you'll be living your purpose.

If you lose your way, progress stalls, and your satisfaction dips. Follow your purpose to find your way back. You'll start making progress again and bring back satisfaction.

GIVING PAVES THE ROAD TO PROGRESS

Jim won a project to build a middle-income housing community. He had to deal with City Hall red tape and whims of its staff. Tom, the zoning officer, was hard-nosed about some minor building code issues, slowing down the project to the point that the construction crew was spending whole days sitting around waiting for approvals to resume work. Jim had already lost a lot of money, but confronting Tom would make matters worse.

One day while waiting for some paperwork at City Hall, Jim learned that a local non-profit school building had caught fire. A teenage prank started it. The non-profit taught vocational skills to the south side youth to help them get jobs, steering them away from drugs and crime. The non-profit survived on little state funding and some donations from the residents. The property insurance they could afford didn't fully cover the loss. Without classes starting back soon, the state funding could stop, risking such a great cause.

Jim admired what the school did for the city youth and decided to help. Using his available crew and his bulk discount for materials, Jim knew he could repair the building for much less than other contractors.

He drove to the location. On his way, he called his crew, who agreed to help. When he reached the school and jumped out of his truck, he saw Tom chatting with the non-profit staff. There was a strange expression on Tom's face when he saw Jim. Tom was cynical at first when Jim offered to help. Jim assured him that he'd take care of the repairs and restore the property at much less cost. Though doubtful, Tom involved him in the discussions with the non-profit and the city staff to start the repair process. Tom knew that the options were limited and the school could use all the help they could get. To his surprise, Jim's crew arrived within the hour to assess the damage and plan the repair. Within a week the classes resumed.

Tom couldn't thank Jim enough for helping out. The mayor asked Jim to attend a special reception and honored him with a Community Angel Award.

Jim was now a friend of the town, not just another contractor. He had support from City Hall, and Tom advised him on how to stay compliant and avoid costly delays. As a result, his project approvals came much faster, he progressed quickly and completed the community housing project ahead of schedule — resulting in a fat bonus from the builder.

Giving has the power to remove obstacles and motivate others to help you make progress in what you set out to achieve.

CHAPTER 6

THE SECOND, REAR BALANCING WHEEL

SATISFACTION IS ONE of the rear supporting wheels on your tricycle, but it needs a balancing wheel for stability as you ride through the journey of life and make it fun. That balancing wheel is Smiles. Both rear wheels hinge on the core values of Authenticity, Gratitude, Purpose, and Giving.

> *You must stay authentic, rested, and connected with your inner self so you can smile when the opportunity presents itself.*

Smiles take two forms, which originate from different parts of the brain. The Duchenne smile, named after a French researcher, is the genuine smile that raises the cheeks and creates crinkles around the eyes. I call it smiling with your eyes — your face and spirits shine. The say-cheese fake smile is merely an upturned mouth.

You smile when you carry the purity of a child within. You smile when you appreciate what you have, and give with an open heart. When you are authentic, rested, and connected with your inner self, you smile at every opportunity.

When you wake up thinking of all the new possibilities and opportunities for adventure and fun, your day starts with a real smile.

KEEPING YOUR FRAME RUST-FREE BRINGS SMILES

When you are inauthentic, you're busy covering things up. That takes your smile away. Or if you do smile, it's fake. Being your real self, you aren't stressed to prove anything. You don't mince words or mislead anyone. You feel free. When you have reasons to smile, you do — genuinely.

A colleague from one of my first consulting assignments in the United States believed he could fake his way through life. He wore a fake smile and tried to fit in and impress others. He scored a few wins but ruined many more relationships — with relatives, friends, and business partners. No one trusted him or wanted to deal with him. When he woke up to his losses, he realized authenticity was key. It took some time for others to believe he was being genuine, but he's on his way now to rebuilding his life. He has fixed some of his relationships — and his reputation too. Though it may be a long ride, he feels liberated and is already enjoying more smiles.

GRATITUDE AND PURPOSE LEAD TO SMILES

Counting your blessings every day will nurture your soul, and you'll respond to the smallest reasons to smile. When others help you, feeling gratitude will allow you to thank them with a real smile — the return gift. And that genuine smile can make someone's day.

Knowing exactly where you are heading allows you to enjoy the journey with a confident smile on your face.

If your life and career are all over the place and you're unclear about where you're going and what's next, it's tough to smile. Finding and aligning your life with purpose invites you to look at every day as full of possibilities. Knowing exactly where you're heading allows you to enjoy the journey with a confident smile on your face.

My wife heals others as a holistic nutritionist and health coach. By staying focused on her purpose, she has changed many lives with her gifts. She feels blessed and full of gratitude for the higher power behind her ability to help others. Those who meet her notice right away that she is all smiles.

PEDALING HARD BRINGS SMILES

When you are not in a race, yet pedal hard to move your tricycle ahead, you smile. You did as a child, and you can do it now.

When you give and see how it benefits others, it motivates you to give more, to pedal faster. Others admire you, are attracted to you, and want to join you. Giving fills both giver and receiver with positive energy. When everyone is feeling good, the floodgates of genuine smiles open wide.

THE SIMPLICITY SPOKE OF SMILES WHEEL

The Smiles wheel has two key spokes—Simplicity and Bliss. Simplicity is the quality or condition of anything which allows you to easily understand it, use it, and fix any problems with it.

Imagine you are a product you see at a mall—one with many features, each activated by pressing a combination of buttons on the front panel. After testing a few buttons, if it looks complicated, who would buy you? I wouldn't. But what if you offer a few — but essential — functions and your few core features work every time with simple instructions?

Simplicity can make you an instant hit. People will like you, use your services, and recommend you to others.

Children live one day at a time and are honest in telling you how they feel about something. They're happy playing with only a block of wood or a ball. They are curious but seek a simple answer. They show their frustration or excitement without a filter and ask when they need attention. They live with simplicity.

Simplify who you are, what you have on your mind, and how you frame your life. Hack away at unnecessary and unwanted objects and thoughts. Determine what you don't need by using your inner lens rather than the world's expectations. Making choices all the time is draining. Reduce both the options you choose from and those you offer to others.

While you clean up the physical and mental clutter, get rid of some other habits. Don't delay or push things off until tomorrow. Items that you never cross off your to-do list create stress and add to the confusion. And don't make promises or take on projects beyond your ability and availability — they can crush you.

I now live by two rules:

- Fewer things are done Better
- Things fly when you Simplify

These mantras also guide my team.

A senior marketing leader wanted to learn about how we help as an IT thought leadership media company. To our peril, she joined the call and announced that she had only ten minutes. I had joined the web meeting to listen in. I knew my team would struggle since they had received training to deliver such presentations in 45-60 minutes. Given the situation, I stepped in and completed in seven minutes and 50 seconds.

"Beautiful! I've been in this industry for many years. You've done a great job in making your offerings simple, elegant, and well thought out. I'm interested in a pilot campaign." The time crunch brought the best and the most straightforward explanation out of me. And it worked.

Wish to have enough, not all.

Whatever you do in your life should lead you to what you want—whether sales numbers, more time for your hobbies, vacations with the family, or exercising to stay healthy. You can realize your dreams by simplifying both work and personal life.

Simplicity can pave the path for professional growth and boost your career. Simplicity helps you bring clarity and find the time so you can focus on career options that draw on your natural talent. As a result, you deliver elegant solutions that add value to those you serve.

Wish to have enough—not all. Reduction in life doesn't mean you must cut to the bone. It means being comfortable with the time, space, and energy you have that allow you to do things that matter. It's about simplicity, not sacrifice.

Let simplicity create breathing room so you can enjoy the pleasant flavors of life.

HOW CAN YOU FIND SIMPLICITY?

Start paring down stuff at home, items you carry when you travel, and thoughts in your head. Unclutter what claims your attention each day. Observe how you approach solving problems and dealing with situations. Can you bow out of the unnecessary projects and priorities that you're juggling because you said *Yes* without considering the rest of your life?

Practice daily subtraction toward simplicity. Discard the stuff you don't need. Strike off items from your wish list that take your focus away from what's important to you. Do the same with tasks, projects, and even some toxic relationships that don't nourish you. Say *No* to anything that would add complexity to your life.

You don't need the most advanced smartphone to be productive. Buying a luxury electric car won't earn you the earth-savior award. Rare collections or big homes won't increase your self-esteem. Having a bigger bed won't lead to better sleep—simplicity will.

How do you explain what you do for a living, or the

concept behind something you built, or how you create value? How do you express your feelings toward someone who matters? Do you use too many or complicated words? Make your thoughts, tasks, creations, and explanations easy to understand and consider. When faced with a problem, don't solve it with the first solution that comes to mind. Look for the most straightforward answer — which in most cases is the most elegant one.

Leading with authenticity removes temptations and mental clutter. It enables simplicity.

When purpose drives you, every possibility doesn't seem like an opportunity. Use your purpose as a filter to prevent clutter and to focus on what you must think, plan, and do. Purpose gives clarity and reason for what stays or goes. Ahh...more simplicity.

I coached a successful entrepreneur whose business grew tenfold in just a few years. To build up his company further, he was looking for ways to increase the number of services offered. When we met, he was feeling stretched and confused by trying to deal with this expansion effort.

He admitted that his success so far was the result of sticking to his formula — few customers, fewer offerings, and excellent delivery. Though the new services he wanted to launch were hot, he and his team lacked the skills and background, so he was nervous, struggling to figure out how to go to market with the new offerings. And since he was too busy handling current operations, he had no time for the expansion effort. On top of everything else, he had announced his ambitious plans among his friends. Now he felt pressure to save face.

We discussed how being inauthentic had complicated his life. He'd taken on too much, and now was trying to live up to other people's expectations. The business growth could come from the well-planned addition of customers and services —without losing simplicity.

He agreed to stay authentic and commit to simplicity. As a result, his business continues to grow, and he's enjoying the journey with a lot more smiles.

THE BLISS SPOKE OF SMILES WHEEL

Are you always busy dealing with your duties and making money? Have you crushed the child inside who wants to feel alive and have fun?

Your inner being is like a battery. If it loses charge, you can't respond well to hardships or enjoy what's uplifting in your life. Keep checking your internal battery. If it's running out of juice, it's time to recharge it. And you can do it with Bliss, the second spoke of the Smiles wheel.

Bliss is the feeling of pure joy when you live priceless moments that charm you. In those moments you're looking beyond the flaws in life. You're not worrying about gain or loss. When you're feeling bliss, nothing else matters—and you lose track of time.

Do you remember the feeling of dancing to your favorite song with your friends? Or ocean waves clapping against your bare feet at the beach as you watch the sunset? Or your head buzzing with freshness after a good night's sleep? That's bliss.

It was bliss watching my son leading a prayer meeting at his Tae Kwon Do graduation ceremony when he got his first belt. And seeing my daughter's first dance recital at the annual school concert.

If you pause your busy life occasionally and enjoy bliss, it will lead to more smiles in your life. Next time you're on your way to a business appointment, take a few minutes to add bliss to your day. Break your routine.

Bliss doesn't need to wait for your
budget or vacation schedule.

Take your nose off the grindstone and jump on your tricycle to explore new roads and unfamiliar scenery. Exit the freeway on a long business trip to watch the sunset from the edge of an open field. Stop on your way back from a working lunch to listen to the peppy music of street performers. Hum along, move to the beat. When back in the office, feel the burst of energy and the broad smile on your face.

What did you like doing as a child? Try bringing some of those activities back into your life. They lead to bliss.

Bliss doesn't need to wait for your budget or vacation schedule. You can find bliss in your home, backyard, office, even the daily commute. Sitting in your pajamas, eating a favorite snack, and reading an absorbing novel can be bliss.

Keep filling your life with bliss, and you'll be like a fresh-water fountain for the thirsty. People will want to be with you. They'll be ready to work for you and follow you. Bliss will keep your internal battery fully charged. You'll go after your goals with high energy and handle problems with confidence — producing results that exceed expectations.

When you're faking it or wearing a mask, you're busy covering things up, which drains away your ability to find bliss in daily life. Staying authentic allows you to be yourself and enjoy bliss whenever the opportunity arises.

In the act of giving, you're open and light-hearted. You're enjoying the moment. You want to help others and bring them happiness. They wish to be happy too, so they join in. Acts of giving, alone or as part of a group, lead to priceless moments of bliss.

I once chaired an IT leadership conference session at an exotic beach resort on the West Coast. The highlight was the outdoor cocktail reception with a beautiful ocean view. I met a successful software company executive who kept harping on some issues which were holding him back from launching the new release of the product line he was managing.

After fifteen minutes of listening to his rant, I excused myself to enjoy the fantastic natural beauty. Later, I overheard him sharing his miseries with another person. He told me he had experienced a high growth path in the company, and his children were doing well in college. But he was only focused on what wasn't going well. Because he lacked gratitude, he was unable to enjoy even a few moments of bliss.

People who only count what they don't have, you'll find them just whining, complaining, and fighting the life they have. Be grateful for your gifts. It will let you put your struggles aside and enjoy being in the moment when you have an opportunity to experience bliss.

Jim arrived home on a Friday evening from a week-long business trip. After he settled down and had dinner, Sue knew he'd ask for coffee before they'd sit together and catch up on what happened while he was gone.

"So, how was the trip?" Sue asked, handing the coffee cup to Jim.

"The meetings went OK. I have some follow-up calls to make next week. But I can't stop thinking about the taxi driver who dropped me at home today." Jim stretched his feet on the recliner. "It wasn't a limousine service, but he offered me water when I sat down and asked how the flight was. I've never had a taxi driver show such courtesy."

"Guess you were lucky, Jim." Sue picked up her cup and lounged next to him.

"On the way home, he shared how he came to the United States. Because of war at home he arrived as a refugee with only a bag of clothes. That's it. But somehow, in a few months he got his driver's license, arranged for a rental taxi, and now he's working the airport-to-city circuit, hauling travelers like me. He's also attending the community college on his way to a bachelor's degree.

"What's impressive was his attitude. He kept sharing stories about the famous landmarks along the highway. There were a few that even I didn't know, though I'm a native here. It's his daily route, but he seemed so full of life, thrilled to share what he saw as if it was his first time."

"Now that's one rare taxi driver, for sure," Sue said with a chuckle.

"You're right. I asked about his positive attitude toward life despite leaving his home country, working eighteen hour shifts driving, and also studying. His response is still ringing in my ears.

"He said, 'America is beautiful, the people here are lovely, and what happened to me doesn't change that. I'm grateful to be alive, have a job, and be able to study.

Many in my country couldn't escape. They died. My life will be what I make of it. I know it's going to be tough, but I take the time to find beauty and enjoy it. It keeps me going.'

"Amazing guy. He taught me a few lessons today." With that, Jim turned on the TV. Sue could see that the taxi driver had left Jim thinking. She knew, as usual, Jim wanted some alone time to wind down before going to sleep.

"I'm going to bed now. Don't start snoring here on the couch. Come soon," Sue said as she got up.

WAYS TO MISS BLISS

If you long for a fancy watch or car, until you buy it, you'll be anxious. But once you have it, you may keep it close to you for only a couple of days. You may swell with pride when others praise it—but that doesn't lead to bliss. Money doesn't buy bliss.

You can find bliss in the simplest of moments.
You need not chase it, lose sleep over it,
or pay a hefty price for it.

Strangely enough, you may even develop a notion that you're not supposed to enjoy bliss every day, that you must wait for the weekend or a vacation. So, you slog nonstop even with a discharged internal battery, depriving yourself of those pleasant moments that make life worth living. And if you catch yourself having a little fun, it fills you up with guilt for not working hard enough.

Once I was at a party talking shop with another guest—an intense intellectual discussion on how important it is to recharge one's batteries to stay in the game and do well every day. "So, what do you do for fun? Any hobbies?" he asked.

The question stumped me. I tried to trace back what I did every day. Jam-packed with calls, emails, and business meetings, even during short breaks, I looked for material to read, to squeeze in more learning. When walking to appointments I called or sent text messages to prospects and my teams. Driving back, I listened to news or podcasts for more knowledge. At home, I went straight to the computer to check off another item on my to-do list, eat dinner, and watch a documentary to improve my awareness. Where was fun? Was I trying to become Obi-Wan Kenobi?

FILLING YOUR LIFE WITH BLISS

It's surprisingly easy to find bliss. You need not chase it, lose sleep over it, or pay a hefty price for it.

As you go through your journey, you can enjoy many moments of bliss by occasionally putting your smartphone down and hitting the pause button on your busy life.

A. MAKING DAILY BLISS A PRIORITY

Ask a family member or partner to remind you to pause. Or use an alarm. Set aside a few minutes to be with the family with no interruption. Go out for a walk alone, with your spouse, or with co-workers. Invite others who value bliss to walk with you and build this habit.

B. **JOURNALING BLISS**

Use your phone or a notebook to capture what you've done that brought you bliss—and how it felt. Once a week, read it to figure out what works. You'll build a system to make bliss a part of your daily life.

C. **HELPING OTHERS ENJOY BLISS**

Can you do something for or with your family, friends, or co-workers to help them experience bliss? To someone lost or caught in an endless chase, bliss can serve as a balm to soothe a bruised soul. And helping others with bliss may help you experience it yourself more often.

Bliss is now part of my life—though it's still hectic. But now I try to steal moments alone or with my family to recharge. I try to schedule extra downtime between appointments, so there's no rush. You can find me at a farmer's market when I'm downtown for business meetings. When traveling, I no longer order room service or call it a night early. Instead, I go out and explore the city.

For me bliss is also having a good home-cooked meal for lunch on the weekend, then crashing on the couch, putting on a classic movie and dozing off, then waking up hoping to have tea and halwa—an Asian Indian delicacy. To have my wife make it, begging her, being a good boy, and making her laugh—is also bliss.

CHAPTER 7

THE BIG FRONT WHEEL

SUCCESS IS USUALLY the primary focus since it seems to propel us ahead in life. But this big front wheel is the last part out of the box because, in *The Tricycle Way*, it's just a high you experience when you reach your goals.

Nothing is wrong with going after success — it's exciting and may allow you a few luxuries — but it shouldn't be at the cost of satisfaction and smiles. If you only care about success, it's like riding an unbalanced, awkward unicycle.

I knew of an entrepreneur who started his business when he was just 22 and grew it to a $350 million company. To expand further, he merged with other companies and went public. Overnight the company's market value reached billions.

One year later — due to the internet bubble bursting in early 2000 and some bad decisions — the company faced a huge loss. He took a lot of loans to keep it afloat, but the situation went from bad to worse. He had to sell the company for less than $100 million. Even under new ownership, the company kept losing money. The entrepreneur repurchased it after two years for under $10 million and was able to grow the value back again to $80 million. But during this crazy journey, he got a divorce, took drugs, and finally lost his life to a heart attack. He was 45. It was one heck of a journey.

Did the entrepreneur see success? Maybe so. Did he bounce back from multiple failures? Sure. Did he have satisfaction and smiles in his life? Don't think so. Would you like such a ride?

It's okay to go after success. But should you be a power boater who rushes to the target and keeps missing out on the fun? In the race to success, what's getting burned on the back burner? How about being a sailor who reaches the destination a little more slowly, but enjoys the pleasures of the wild, enormous sea? Wouldn't you prefer a balance of success, satisfaction, and smiles for the long journey?

Pause what you're doing and imagine what it would be like to achieve a goal you have in mind. Visualize what you would gain and barriers it would remove for you. Also, the confidence it would build in you to go after the next milestone.

See yourself living that journey—with both the challenges and the benefits.

Painting a vivid picture of the outcome can lead you to push hard to make it a reality. Staying focused on the end state helps you dream through the obstacles and hard work needed to gain knowledge, skills, and experience. You envision the way to build the connections who will help create opportunities. Now, what if you make daily satisfaction and more smiles a priority while you work toward success?

When you become intentional about daily satisfaction and more smiles, not only does the success taste better, it makes the journey easier and fun.

You can plan the shortest route from point A to point B. You can even define the what, when, where, and how. When you start, though, there may be detours and delays. If you steer your tricycle with the handlebar of purpose, you'll find your way back. And the cushioned seat of gratitude will allow you to keep calm during delays.

> **You don't Get *Success*. It's *what you*
> Receive *when you* Give.**

If circumstances force you to follow a choppy path to success with many stops and delays, that's not a failure. Keep going. Don't bother your head with what others will think about delays. Focus on Progress. Get creative and find work-arounds for the snags or limitations.

Success isn't something you can buy. You don't *get* success. Success is what you *receive* when you *give*.

NINE MYTHS ABOUT SUCCESS

1. SUCCESS IS ONLY MATERIAL

Fact: Success means more than money or fame. Do you value success in *all* the critical areas of your life? Loss and disappointment are easy to find if you chase only material success.

2. SUCCESS MEANS HAVING LOTS OF FANS AND FOLLOWERS

Fact: Success is not about showing off or make-believe. If you have a positive impact on a few people who trust you, and you matter in their lives—that's real success.

3. SUCCESS IS OVERNIGHT

Fact: Success depends on years of daily commitment and attention—giving, as well as creating value for others.

4. SUCCESS MEANS NO MISTAKES

Fact: Success comes to those who aren't afraid of slip-ups and failures. Be experimental. Blunders can make you aware of what you didn't know. If you fall off your horse, dust yourself off, and take a vow to get back on.

5. SUCCESS REQUIRES FOCUSING ON YOUR OWN NEEDS FIRST

Fact: It's others who make you successful. Concentrate on what they need and how you deliver it. Exceed their expectations.

6. **SUCCESS REQUIRES BEING OPPORTUNISTIC**

Fact: Opportunists chase whatever they think will help them get ahead. They may enjoy an occasional win, but maximum success comes from aligning with your purpose. Use purpose as the lens to review all opportunities that come your way—and help focus your time, energy, and resources.

7. **SUCCESS IS ALL ABOUT MANIPULATION AND POLITICS**

Fact: If you play politics or manipulate others, you'll never earn trust. Stay authentic about your intentions and capabilities while speaking to others, as well as in all your actions and interactions.

8. **SUCCESS REQUIRES SACRIFICING ME TIME**

Fact: You must keep developing yourself and innovate as part of serving others. Investing in me time is critical to allow you to recharge your batteries, sharpen your saw, and keep connected with your inner self.

9. **SUCCESS REQUIRES PROPER EDUCATION AND BACKGROUND**

Fact: Many people raised in low-income families achieve success with little or no formal training. Formal education can widen your general knowledge and perspective of how the world works. But don't let this gap hold you back. Start from where you are. Let life educate you.

People may suggest that you play safe, advising against walking less traveled paths. Some might even ridicule you for breaking norms. But you're better off being seen as foolish and stupid while you go after seemingly impossible goals. Blaze a new trail — you'll not only enjoy the daily satisfaction and more smiles but also reach greater heights of success.

Inventors, freedom fighters, and other heroes we admire didn't know up front if they would succeed by taking risks. But they refused to live in the status quo and didn't wait for a perfect time to act. Driven by purpose, they charged ahead with courage and confidence, to work despite hardships and roadblocks.

Henry Ford said *whether you think you can, or you think you can't — you're right*. It isn't what others say you are or can be — it's what you believe. If others see you as rebellious, rash, or wild, it doesn't matter. It's your journey to enjoy with a purpose to fulfill.

CORE VALUES FOR SUCCESS

Success involves developing excellence in how you deliver. In being authentic, you are your harshest critic. You don't cut corners even when no one is looking. You don't cover up your mistakes or weaknesses by saying things that aren't true. You let others see you as you are — they'll admire you and trust you to serve their needs.

Becoming and staying successful is a hard and long journey. Gratitude keeps your energy and morale high, and helps you deal with accepting and coping with challenges along the way.

With a clear purpose, you're not distracted. It helps you focus on things that align with your calling. You might find strength by concentrating on fewer associates, skills, and projects.

Work toward success with the intention of giving. Don't bother to keep score or deliver only so much as you're getting in return. Instead, commit yourself to creating the most value for others. When others get more than they sign up for, they'll keep coming back to you for their needs — and bring their friends along.

SPOKES OF SUCCESS WHEEL

Three Spokes keep the integrity and strength of the Success Wheel. They are Relationships, Branding, and Performance.

1. **RELATIONSHIPS:** Don't you have a few friends, peers, or customers who you'd like to help prosper because of the bond you have with them? Build and nurture healthy relationships with people. They'll become your well-wishers, and help you in any way they can to build your success.

2. **BRANDING:** A strong brand allows people to associate you with a skill you have, a service you offer, or your capacity to solve a particular problem. You will pop up in their mind when someone expresses a need, even when you're

not around. As a result, you'll get inquiries and referrals for your services.

3.   **PERFORMANCE:** When you deliver on tasks, make good on your promises, and exceed expectations, your performance builds credibility and opens more doors.

Relationships make others want to help you and see you succeed. Branding keeps you in the front of their mind. And performance instills trust in your abilities. These three spokes, when installed correctly and kept in balance, lead to greater success.

THE RELATIONSHIPS SPOKE OF SUCCESS WHEEL

Alone you can go fast, but take others along to go far. Building strong and healthy relationships is critical to continued success—but it takes time, energy, and trust.

> *People don't care how much you know.*
> *They want to know how much you care.*

People don't care how much you know—they want to know how much you care. See if these practical tips build stronger relationships for you:

- Don't keep score or attach conditions before you invest in relationships.

- In conflict, relationships are always more valuable than situations and things.
- Focus on understanding others before seeking to be understood. Take the time to learn about their wants, needs, cares, and quirks.
- Accept others the way they are. Don't try to change them to your liking.
- Don't wait for special occasions to build healthy relationships. Try to be of value whenever you interact with them. Help where they need you. Create opportunities for them.
- Ease their fears and insecurities. Motivate them and offer them hope.
- Do and say things that make them feel valued. Be intentional about recognizing and appreciating their unique gifts.

Don't measure any relationship based on what you are getting out of it. If you focus on what's lacking, you end up disappointed—and you stop working on the relationship.

"Can we plan our vacation to the Bahamas, Jim? You need a break, too. Should I look for tickets?" Sue asked as they sat down for lunch with Heather.

"Bahamas will have to wait. Crater Tech gave the contract to someone else. I was sure we'd get it after I helped them build a few manufacturing plants. They were happy with my work. Not sure what happened. I just learned about it."

Jim was shocked and disappointed. He had planned to book those tickets once he bagged the Crater Tech contract. Losing it was a massive blow to his hopes as well as his cash flow. His business had been a revolving door since the beginning.

"Not sure what I'm doing wrong here! I'm working my tail off to land these clients. I do my best for them, but they leave me. I watch my competitors getting bigger by the day though they opened their company only a few years ago. It hurts to see my old clients working with them."

"So sorry to hear, Jim. I'm sure you'll bounce back. How's it going with Marty's contract?" Heather was concerned.

"I still have his contract. I'm on it and showing him results." Jim sounded more cheerful.

"That's good. Do you and Marty talk when you meet? Or is it only business?"

"Of course, we talk. We talk business, what else? I'm not sure if he is looking for chitchat, and I'm not interested either. I'm busy delivering what he has asked me to do."

"What have you learned about Marty's life?"

"All I need to know is that he runs this big company that pays its bills. He did invite me to the company picnic, but I bowed out with an excuse that I had a prior commitment. I'm not sure if I should try making friends with him when I don't have much time. With a family to feed and bills piling up, I need to be out there selling —and then delivering on the projects I sell."

"Do you know anyone else at Marty's company?"

"Yeah, I work with a few project managers."

"The project is going well, right?" Heather kept probing.

"Things are never perfect in this business. We had a few slippages which delayed the project, and cost also went up a little. I did mess up a few times, but I got away without having to offer any credit or do extra work for free. You know, I've been around the block." Jim smirked.

"Are you still advising Marty? Does he still come to you for help? I know you impressed him when you guys first met."

"He's reached out maybe a few times since I started helping with the buildout. His VP is responsible for the manufacturing plants, and he asks for my help way more than I like. He dropped by my desk several times this week and wants another meeting again next week. I'm tolerating it, so he doesn't complain to Marty. But I'm planning to set Marty's expectations straight about it. He hired me to finish his construction project. If he wants me to spend any more time with his staff, he needs to hire me on a separate consulting retainer."

"What do you do when you see Marty's staff making any mistakes since you are advising them on other things anyway?"

"It's their problem. I just mind my own business. I don't own that company, and they don't pay me extra. Should I care?" Jim snapped. He wasn't interested in the conversation, but he respected Heather, so he kept responding.

"Is this how you deal with all your clients?"

"What do you mean? What else am I supposed to do? The clients pay me to get their job done. This is business. They are not my friends. I'm better off keeping my distance and doing the work they pay me for."

"I'll be right back. Let me get a cup of coffee. Sue, Jim, do you want some?" Heather wanted to process what she heard and let Jim cool off before offering him advice.

"I'll come with you, Heather. Let me brew a fresh pot." Sue could sense that the discussion got a little heated and wanted to leave Jim alone.

"When we go back, Sue, pay attention to what I tell Jim since you're also looking to grow your customers."

"Sure." Sue also felt that there were issues with how Jim was running his business, but she didn't know how to help him. She'd seen Jim working hard day and night, but the company never reached a point with stable clients.

Once Heather and Sue brought back coffee and sat down facing Jim, Heather took a deep breath and started addressing Jim in a tone that meant strictly business.

"Based on what I heard, Jim, you are breaking all the rules of building business relationships. If you treat your other clients the same way you treat Marty and his team, no wonder it's a revolving door.

"Marty trusted you based on a five-minute chat with him at a party and awarded you this big contract. It could be the start of a long-term association." Heather was reminding Jim of how a small act of giving had helped him.

"I know. That's what I'm doing with other people I meet—and it's working. I'm very close to bringing a few new customers on board."

"Here's the issue, Jim. Marty respects you for your knowledge and experience. That's why his team comes to you for help. But you're counting minutes when they do, looking to get even more money out of them. You have a lot to offer, and sharing what you know will only bring them closer to you.

"Marty may be your client, but he's also a person with his own needs, vision, and desires. The same is true for his staff. If you took the time to learn about them as people, wouldn't that help you manage their expectations, handle situations, and maybe resolve their conflicts? As a general contractor, isn't that what you get paid to do?

"When your client wins, you win, Jim. These clients always have vendors knocking on their door for business, but they want a partner who understands their needs, can solve their problems, and can be trusted. Have you been that partner for your customers? If you were, do you think they would've left you?" Heather took a deep breath.

For a few minutes, there was total silence in the room. It was clear from the expression on his face that Heather's comments had rattled Jim.

"You're right, Heather. If I hadn't messed up, I'd still

have all my customers with me today. I've been chasing new clients but forgetting the ones I already had. I never built relationships and so I guess I paid the price. I'll work on fixing this. Thanks again, Heather. Not sure what I'd do without you," Jim said with a sheepish smile.

AUTHENTICITY IN RELATIONSHIPS

Trust is the foundation for all relationships. If you bend the tricycle's frame — which is your authenticity — to turn odds in your favor, others lose faith in you. Staying authentic gains and keeps trust.

A large manufacturing company in the United States was struggling to fill a senior IT position. Their internal recruiters and existing staffing vendors gave up after six months of effort. Through a recommendation, their VP reached out to ask if my IT consulting firm could help.

We interviewed the hiring manager and discovered issues with the job description and the top salary offered. It was a self-inflicted problem. Aiming only to please, neither their internal staff nor vendors stepped up to expose the issues.

We stayed authentic and reported our findings: areas where the client executives and HR were off track. Sharing current market data about available skill mix and salary levels, we helped them correct course. Using our national executive network, we filled the position within four weeks. It was the start of a great relationship with this client, and now they keep asking us to help with additional hires—and recommend us to their partners.

Want to build and keep strong personal relationships?

Base them on authenticity. Be open and honest and share what the other person must hear. Sugarcoating comments or withholding feedback causes more harm than good.

Heather announced one day that her dad was having some health issues. She needed to visit him and could be gone more than a few weeks. But she promised Jim and Sue to return as soon as she could.

With Heather gone, there was no one to vent at and help discuss the issues. Tensions started mounting. Soon Jim and Sue were just tolerating each other. There were no fights—only a lot of silence and compromise. They were on speaking terms but had drifted apart.

A few days later, after Jim's close friend Joe got married, the newlyweds invited Jim and Sue and a few other couples over for a party. Jim and Sue couldn't refuse since Joe had been the best man at their wedding.

After drinks and dinner, Joe moved everyone to the family room for a few games. One of them required everyone to share five things they liked about their life partner and five things they disliked. It was an odd moment for both Jim and Sue. They tried to slip out but finally surrendered.

Sue started first with five appreciations. When listing what she disliked about Jim, Sue found herself explaining why she thought Jim did those things. Listening to her, Jim decided to do the same when it was his turn to talk about Sue.

Though others joked about what they'd said about

each other, Jim and Sue both realized how well each understood the other, accepting their flaws. On the drive home, as a loving couple, they talked about how not being open with each other had strained their relationship. They promised to stay open and honest.

GRATITUDE ENHANCES RELATIONSHIPS

Do you take your significant other or business partners for granted? Do you only appreciate them for what they do for you?

Let gratitude, the cushioned seat of your tricycle, be the glue to help strengthen the bond. Gratitude puts into focus the good qualities in individuals and why you engaged with them initially. You appreciate them and feel blessed for having them in your life.

Gratitude makes you value these relationships and willingly nurture them. You try to do things they like, and that signal motivates them to do the same.

Though there may be times when you can't stand each other, valuing each other for what you got from the relationship dissolves sourness and moves you to restore the bond.

GIVING IS THE KEY TO CONNECTIONS

Doing only as much as you get paid for is a transaction. Creating value where you aren't expecting any additional compensation or returning any favor conveys that you care. You gain respect and make a deeper connection with those you serve. It's giving that pedals your tricycle ahead.

Over the years many of my customers have become friends. We no longer sell or buy. We meet for coffee or catch up by phone every few months. When they share their personal or professional problems, we have a candid discussion. I ask questions to understand their issues and offer objective advice or honest feedback. As appropriate, I make professional introductions or suggest useful resources with the sole intent of helping them. Guess who they call when they need help in my area of expertise?

Be a giver in all relationships.

It wasn't always like this for me. I once visited a corporate CIO at her office. We met every few months and enjoyed catching up. There were potential consulting opportunities at her company. After some small talk, I asked her if there was a way we could support any of her projects. There wasn't at the moment, but she suggested that we stay in touch.

We had only spent half the time scheduled for the meeting when I picked up my coat and started to leave. I know the CIO realized that I was playing the sales guy—not the friend she thought I was. She stayed courteous and walked me, face down, all the way to the door. When I tried to restart small talk, she mumbled a few words in response. I had destroyed a great relationship trying to get business from her.

Contrast this to now. I met a senior IT director at his office to discuss the career day program I run for college students, where volunteer IT managers roleplay the real world of

IT with them. He agreed to volunteer. He also opened up, sharing his ambitions and asking for career advice. I gave him some tips and offered to refine his résumé. I shared some best practices related to IT team building and talent retention, and our long conversations continued over the phone. Later he invited my firm to help with critical hires and recommended us to others. Focused on nurturing our relationship, I don't have to ask for opportunities. But the text messages arrive: *I need to hire some people—call me.*

ACCEPTANCE IMPROVES RELATIONSHIPS

No two people are the same in their thinking, habits, and beliefs. Your spouse could be a clean freak. A customer may always demand printed reports vs. emailed documents. Don't let their quirks demotivate you from investing in the relationship. Don't try to change them to your preferences. Accept it all as part of their personalities and support them to improve as per their will, in ways that fit their style. Accepting differences doesn't make you a sucker—it helps build relationships.

Like any couple, my wife and I have our differences. In the earlier years of our marriage, our heated arguments could have won awards on reality TV. It was only frustration over why one person doesn't behave to the other's liking. Over time we learned to accept each other's quirks and developed a strong bond. Now we stand together, united, no matter what curveballs life throws at us.

FOCUS ON PROGRESS SUPPORTS RELATIONSHIPS

Relationship building is somewhat like parenting teenagers. It takes ongoing effort and patience. What you say or don't say, do or don't—everything has an impact.

Don't expect overnight results—it will only cause frustration. Stay focused on progress. Keep investing in the relationship, look for signs of positive change, and get feedback on what you might do better to improve the connection.

I've been working with a global conference organizer for many years. They trust me as a professional event chair and moderator to make their executive events interactive and engaging. And I admire and have confidence in their company leadership. I always strive to exceed their expectation by helping to further their business agenda.

The relationship went through turbulent times that tested the bond, but I kept investing, staying focused on progress. Our mutual respect and trust have deepened. I moderate many of their global events, and we continue to strengthen our partnership.

SIMPLICITY HELPS WITH RELATIONSHIPS

Are you looking to build or fix a relationship? Begin by developing clarity about expectations and how you'll interact and handle conflicts. Invest in simplicity. It pays handsome dividends.

In business, that includes contract terms, milestones, and deliverables. At home, it's usually about how everyone talks and behaves, who'll drop the kids at soccer or dance practice, what triggers their timeouts—and what's going to put me in the doghouse.

BLISS BOOSTS RELATIONSHIPS

Enjoying bliss makes life worth living. It recharges your internal battery, so you put more into your relationships.

I took my wife to a resort in Philadelphia for our honeymoon, but she hated it. So, we canceled the booking, rented a car, and drove to New York with no hotel reservations.

On another occasion, her stylist bailed out at the last moment as she was getting ready for a Christmas party. I practically broke into a salon and negotiated with the owner for her hairdo.

Before starting our family, we spent many Friday evenings hanging out together as a couple, having cocktails, moving to the beat of some peppy songs, and cooking each other's favorite dishes.

These were among the many moments that brought us closer and made our bond stronger. Time has put our relationship to the test, but bliss keeps us together.

One of my friends likes to meet his prospects and customers in a personal setting. He keeps it casual with no business agenda and ensures that everyone has a great time, including himself. All his customers remember him for the blissful moments they've shared. The deep personal bonds he creates result in many long-term clients who love working with him.

THE BRANDING SPOKE OF SUCCESS WHEEL

Branding is about developing your industry standing in the area of your expertise. It differentiates you from others. If you build a strong brand, people care about what you say, support your mission, reach out for your services, and refer others to you.

> *You don't become a brand*
> *— others make you one.*

You don't become a brand—others make you one. Serve with your unique talent and solve problems better than others. Keep at it to build a strong personal brand.

There are no shortcuts in branding—it takes many years and ongoing hard work, learning, and creativity. Don't fall for making false claims or twisting facts to speed the process. Such tactics do more harm than good.

Knowing your purpose makes the branding journey easier. Following your purpose, with passion and talent, you go all out, learning, innovating, and sharing your knowledge and experience with the world. This creates recognition for your unique gifts and boosts your brand.

Strong branding is a reward you earn for your selfless giving. Use your talents to help the needy, even at no cost. Or teach other people in your trade how to improve their skills. When your support and giving helps people grow, they lift you even higher.

There is even a side benefit: as people notice how much you give, they will spread the word about it and inspire others to use your services.

Branding, like relationships, takes time, ongoing work, and grit. It's like building a castle — one brick at a time. Staying focused on progress helps keep your spirits high during the journey. Michelangelo could see beautiful sculptures in blocks of marble. Exercising patience and making daily progress, he chiseled out his place as one of the greatest sculptors of all time.

Even with a passion for interior design and her hard work, Sue wasn't attracting clients. Most people in the community knew her only as Jim's wife. They liked her jolly nature, invited her to their parties, and admired her for going after her dreams. But she wasn't getting referrals.

She wanted to design interiors for nurseries, childcare centers, and other living spaces for children. But better-known designers in her city kept getting all the contracts. As a newcomer, she was having a tough time convincing people to trust her with their projects. Desperate and anxious to build a customer base, she started saying yes to any business she could get.

"I started with a dream, but I'm not sure if I'll ever see it become a reality. It's much harder than I thought. I'm getting nowhere. My friends know I'm a good interior designer, but they've yet to send a single client my way. No one cares." She poured her heart out to Heather over lunch.

"I want people to know me as the interior designer who can turn any space for children into a beautiful and fun place where kids enjoy being kids."

"That's a beautiful dream, Sue. How much do people, beyond your circle of close friends, know about you and your unique talent? Have they seen any of your work?"

"How do I show my talent when no one is ready to hire me as a designer? It's what I am waiting for—a chance."

"Let me go off topic for a second. When Emily is sick, why do you always call that doctor who practices on the south side of the city? There are many doctors close by."

"Oh, are you referring to Dr. Melanie? I always call her because she's the best. She has a lot of knowledge. Most of my friends in the neighborhood trust her with their kids as well. She was the guest speaker at our mothers' club meeting. The tips she gave are such a great help when Emily is down with a cold. Whenever I meet her, I learn something new about keeping kids healthy.

And she's been running a free clinic for south side children every Sunday for over ten years. Even when she's under the weather, she shows up because these kids depend on her."

"Would you recommend her if someone asks for a good doctor for their children?"

"Yes, of course. There's no one better for kids."

"Sue, do you know why you feel this way about Dr. Melanie? It's because she has built a strong personal brand. She keeps learning, openly shares her knowledge, goes the extra mile to treat her patients, and serves the broader community. What are you willing to do to build such a strong brand?"

"I'm not sure what it'll take, but I'm up for it. I get your point — I'm already hoping customers will line up before there's much to show for my talent. That makes me realize it's a bad idea to go after any and every project I find. Guess I got desperate and lost my focus. Let me make a quick note to call Colbe Brothers as soon as I get to the office — I'll bow out from their office design bid.

"I'm also going to say yes to a local church. The pastor's assistant called me two days ago to see if I'd volunteer to redesign their daycare. Here's another idea. I'll speak to Dr. Melanie to see if I can design interiors for the parents who visit her Sunday clinic. For free, of course. I'm sure they'll love it." Sue was all charged up, poking her salad with excitement and tossing out ideas.

"You got it. This lunch is on me." Heather was glad to see Sue connect the dots.

"Thanks, Heather. For the lunch and the advice!"

BE YOUR TRUE SELF WHEN BUILDING YOUR BRAND

Your brand is a promise—to keep it, authenticity is critical. Weak commitments, fake passion, and inflated claims hold you back from building a strong one. Build your brand brick by brick, using authenticity as the mortar.

An IT professional approached me for guidance on how to establish himself as an expert. During conversations, he confessed to bloating his credentials to land contracts, and to copying other people's ideas and calling them his own. He'd made tall claims beyond his capabilities —and couldn't deliver on his promises. In a few years, he had already been in and out of many companies. His fakery kept pulling him back from reaching his goals.

"What's the hurry?" I asked.

"I know a few very experienced professionals in my field who make a lot of money and are always in demand. I want to make lots of money and be famous like them. How else do I go about it?"

"Sorry, there are no shortcuts. Lying about your background and abilities to get there faster is making it worse for you. Those successful professionals worked hard for many years—learning and doing the right things to get to where they are today. You have to start where you are and follow the right steps that will take you where you want to be. Staying true to yourself along the journey is the only way it works." I looked straight into his eyes. Before we went any further, I had to level with him and make sure he was open to going about it the right way.

He kept his promise and worked to advance his skills. He chose projects that helped him grow his knowledge and industry recognition. As a result, he landed his dream job at a very prestigious firm.

BUILD A PURPOSE-DRIVEN BRAND

Let your purpose, the handlebar of your tricycle, help you find that one lane for the branding journey. As you find your focus, the effort will become more natural, and you'll maintain your excitement and the tenacity to keep at it.

Let your purpose fire you up every day.

I used to boast I was going to be a billionaire, but I had no focus. Freelance consulting, selling handmade greeting cards, a healthy food delivery startup, life-balance software —I scrambled through all of them, and all at the same time. My branding was: *He's All Over the Place.*

Now I'm all about helping IT leaders and professionals assemble their tricycles. This purpose drives my consulting firm, media company, speaking, event moderation, and coaching—laying the foundation for a stronger brand.

Let your purpose fire you up every day. Let it drive you to use your best talent to create the most value for those you serve. With a mission, you are eager to learn, experiment, and innovate, seeing setbacks as opportunities to gain more experience and grow.

A purpose-driven brand is fun to build and has staying power.

BUILD YOUR BRAND THROUGH GOOD ACTS

Strong brands *give*. Offer yourself as a resource beyond the services you deliver. Be generous with what and how much you share. It leads to greater exposure, and you stand out among competitors.

People are always looking to solve their problems, curious about what's ahead of the curve and how to prepare for the future. Help them with what they want, sharing your knowledge and discoveries on a one-to-one basis or through online forums and events. This way the world learns about what you know, how you think, and your unique abilities. People will admire and recommend you, share ideas to improve your craft, and support you. When you build an emotional connection with the community and serve by giving, they make you a brand.

I know and admire a keynote speaker and author for how he fought through many setbacks and built a strong personal brand. He battled cancer, multiple crippling accidents, and financial hardships. During his testing journey, he realized what kept him going was his positive attitude.

The world is full of people facing similar hardships, but they're unable to cope. He started helping others develop a positive attitude by sharing his stories of struggle and bouncing back. People noticed his acts of giving—and opportunities started pouring in for speaking, training, and consulting.

Devoted to the cause, he has authored a book, built training seminars, and is now a sought-after professional. His personal story, passion, and knowledge are an inspiration, and by serving others, he's built a strong personal brand.

THE PERFORMANCE SPOKE OF SUCCESS WHEEL

The Performance spoke of the Success wheel is about putting in your absolute best efforts whenever you get an opportunity to serve—and doing it better than anyone else. That's how you keep your promise, exceed expectations, and build trust in your ability to produce.

Things took off for Sue as she worked on her branding. She decorated the daycare at the local church for free and ran free seminars for mothers at the library. With guidance from Dr. Melanie, she helped the south side parents decorate their children's rooms. People started noticing her work. She was featured in local newspapers and interviewed on the community TV channel. Requests for her services began pouring in.

She was getting more business than she could handle. Wanting to cash in, she didn't refuse any opportunity. She was enjoying the limelight and the long list of customers already signed up.

She hired a nanny for Emily so she could handle the demands of her growing business. Jim built a design studio for her at home so she could work after tucking Emily into bed at night.

Her schedule was full of meetings, coffees, lunches, and networking events—leaving little time to work on the projects she landed. To grab even more contracts, she started committing to impossible deadlines. And, to keep those commitments, she started pitching her old designs.

Things were stretching Sue beyond her physical limits. Heather remembered that a client canceled Sue's contract—a couple who signed Sue up for unique interior design for their newborn's room. She had drafted a few ideas, but they lacked creativity and looked like some of her previous work. Since the baby was due soon, the couple was anxious—they needed to have the nursery ready. And they weren't happy with what Sue had shown them. Heather heard Sue raising her voice when she met with the couple at her office.

"You gave me your requirements, and I designed based on them. I know what I'm doing. If you'd like me to keep working on your project, let me do my job!"

The couple canceled the contract the next day.

"Morons!" screamed Sue, slamming the phone. Heather stopped what she was doing, jumped off her chair, and rushed to Sue's office.

"If they want to cancel the contract, so be it. I don't care!" Sue was furious—another customer called to cancel their project.

"Is everything OK, Sue?"

"Don't ask. At first, I wasn't getting any business. And now these clients are canceling contracts on me, one after another. When will I get to relax and enjoy the fruits of my labor?"

"How about a coffee break?" asked Heather, knowing it was time for Sue to realize where she was going wrong. The bleeding had to stop. The relationships Sue built earlier, and the strong brand she developed, brought her contracts. But her professional performance as a designer and a business person needed fixing.

"I can't stand this anymore. Let's get outta here." Sue picked up her coat and walked out. Heather locked the main door and joined her. The café was busy, but they lucked out and found a quiet spot at the back. Sue ordered a large black coffee. She needed it.

"Are you enjoying being in demand?" Heather started the conversation as both settled.

"To tell you the truth, I hate everything that's happening, Heather. With these clients walking away, canceling contracts, it's no fun at all. They're just so demanding and don't seem to like my designs. I'm not sure if they even know what they want."

"Why did you get into interior design, Sue?"

"You know why, Heather. I want to create beautiful spaces for children."

"Is that what you are doing though?"

"What do you mean? Don't you see all the signed contracts?"

"Sue, you were so happy decorating the daycare at the church where you didn't even get paid. The people who visited the church loved what you created. But now, both you and your clients are miserable. You yell at them, and they're canceling your contracts. You're not doing what you said you love — creating original designs for places where kids can live and dream.

"I see you rushing through contracts and forcing your customers to accept your old design proposals.

You're missing deadlines and losing clients left and right because they're not getting what you promised.

"You worked hard to build relationships and a strong brand—which led to these contracts. But you'll lose them if you don't get your act together. People trusted you to create unique and beautiful spaces for their kids. And it was your dream as well. Now that you have a chance to live your dream and purpose, are you doing it?"

Sue was on the verge of losing it all because she wasn't focusing on performance.

Outcome alone doesn't measure performance. It's also the experience you offer along the way. Put your best thoughts even in a draft you send for client review. Run a spell check on the first cut of the presentation you send to your boss. Be on time with the documents you promised. Listen to those who you serve, get their feedback, and incorporate it to improve your act.

> *Staying authentic is key*
> *to high performance.*

Performance depends on your abilities—but even more on your focus and intention. It's a marathon—and for that, you must have your mind, body, and spirit focused in one direction and be ready for the long haul. You must perform at your best—at all times. If you've committed, live up to it.

Staying authentic is key to high performance. Be true to yourself as you prepare to perform. Stay genuine about your capabilities, and set reasonable expectations which you are sure to meet and exceed. Powered by authenticity, you'll perform not to impress but to create real value.

Having a purpose helps you plan better, even innovate as you perform. It supports overcoming fear because you focus only on living your purpose, giving your best. People notice that extra edge in your performance, which boosts trust.

Perform with the intention of giving. Don't limit your effort or hold back from going beyond the expected. You'll create the wow effect for those who experience your performance. And to your customers, you'll become a partner —not just another vendor.

I once drove six hours from Chicago to Kentucky to meet a prospective client. I asked for a glass of water as we sat down to discuss the task at hand. Just as we started, I accidentally dropped ice water on my suit. Another time the microphone stopped working as I kicked off a conference as the chair and moderator. Has this happened to you? If you expect everything to be perfect, such interruptions can ruin your performance. Things can go wrong, so accept when they do. Believe in yourself, and your preparation, and go for the kill.

Simplify to supercharge your performance.

For an event in New York, I was to conduct prep calls with the sponsors. With so much going on in my business, I attempted to multitask during those calls. Overworked and distracted, I didn't prepare well for the event—and the outcome disappointed the sponsors.

My workload is no less now, but my team and I leave no stone unturned when it comes to performance. As a result, conference organizers keep inviting me to help with their events.

When performing, don't let unrelated personal or professional issues distract you. As a professional event chair and moderator, I must be mentally present on the job. I have to stay focused on attendees' words and actions as I manage the agenda, breaks, and hecklers—and expectations of the presenters, sponsors, and organizers.

Over the years I've had employee issues, project delays, family arguments the day of or before I travel for my professional engagements. When such things happen, and I'm called to take the stage, I accept what I cannot change—and stay focused on the present.

Simplify to supercharge your performance. Gain clarity about your responsibilities and goals, and remove unnecessary steps. See mistakes as learnings, and setbacks as opportunities to try something new. Keep recharging your batteries by having fun and enjoying moments of bliss throughout the process.

You have all the wheels now, but there is one last thing. The tires were already installed on the wheels when your tricycle box arrived and represent physical and mental health. Don't take this critical aspect of your life for granted. Just as your tricycle needs reliable tires, to assemble a good life and to enjoy the ride, you must keep your physical and mental health in top shape.

Now that you know what came in the box and how the parts fit together, the next step is to learn how to assemble and maintain the tricycle. For that, you need only one tool—the right mindset.

CHAPTER 8

THE TOOL

T**HE MINDSET INCLUDES** your assumptions, beliefs, and notions. These help you accept or reject ideas and options in your life. People have one of two types of mindset: fixed or progressive. To serve as a proper tool for tricycle assembly and maintenance, you need a progressive mindset.

Do you consider self-help books, exploring concepts, and discussions as time wasters? Do you try to play safe by shying away from new challenges? Do you complain and cringe in the face of hardships and setbacks? Do you become defensive or even hostile against critical feedback? If yes, your rigid mindset is preventing you from living your full potential —with Success, Satisfaction, and Smiles.

A progressive mindset carries a positive outlook toward life, treating situations and comments with optimism and an open mind. You seek constant learning and improvement. You aren't afraid of challenges—you see them as opportunities for growth and consider setbacks as setups that will push you ahead.

Having a progressive mindset also means flexibility, willingness to fail, and tolerance of flaws in yourself and others. A progressive mindset includes a conscious effort to understand the why and how of life, and explores ideas that challenge your deep-rooted beliefs.

It may take time to make the shift from a fixed to a progressive mindset. And sometimes elements of fixed mindset creep back in as you go about dealing with life situations. Be intentional about making the shift, keep the company of friends with a progressive mindset, and have patience — you'll always have the tool ready for upkeep of your tricycle.

CHAPTER 9

THE ASSEMBLY

ARMED WITH THE right mindset, you're now ready to assemble your tricycle. Don't rush. Follow the steps with attention to details, and be prepared to learn from mistakes you make in the process. At times the directions may seem confusing or parts don't fit together or seem to be missing. Don't worry — you're just starting out.

Don't try to complete the assembly in a few sittings — no need to stress and feel frustrated. If you feel confused or anxious, walk away to clear your head, then come back to it. It's OK to take advice from others, but you must have the final say on how you assemble and maintain your tricycle.

This tricycle is symbolic. For example, I have shown the connection between the simplicity spoke of the smiles wheel and the performance spoke of the success wheel. And there is a conceptual link. But, don't confuse yourself trying to figure out how a spoke of one wheel connects to the spoke of another.

For reference, here's a quick recap of the parts and how

they depend on each other. If you missed some concepts, refer back to the relevant sections. Start assembling your tricycle in the following order:

1.   FRAME (AUTHENTICITY)

The frame of the tricycle represents Authenticity, the very foundation of your life. It provides strength and integrity. Being inauthentic is like twisting the frame or allowing it to rust. When you see issues with authenticity, fix them promptly. Staying authentic is a choice that will never fail you.

2.   CUSHIONED SEAT (GRATITUDE)

The cushioned seat of the tricycle represents Gratitude. It helps reduce the jarring impact of potholes and bumps you may encounter in your journey. Gratitude doesn't change the road, but it makes the ride pleasant and comfortable. Install the seat ensuring it always has enough cushion by practicing daily gratitude, finding new ways to be thankful, and being grateful for what you may otherwise take for granted. Don't just make lists of things to be grateful for in your daily journal—you must feel your attitude of gratitude.

3. HANDLEBAR (PURPOSE)

The handlebar of the tricycle represents Purpose. It keeps life on track, helping you navigate through stumbling blocks and potholes. Take all the time you need to install the handlebar. Commit to defining your purpose and making a conscious effort to keep everything else aligned with it. If you face situations that create detours, reconnect with your purpose to get back on track.

4. PEDALS (GIVING)

Pedals on the tricycle represent Giving —the way you propel your life forward. The more you pedal, the further you go in life. Install pedals correctly, so no friction prevents you from giving. Practice giving in all the roles you play in life, without keeping score or being selective. Giving isn't an obligation—it's a way of life.

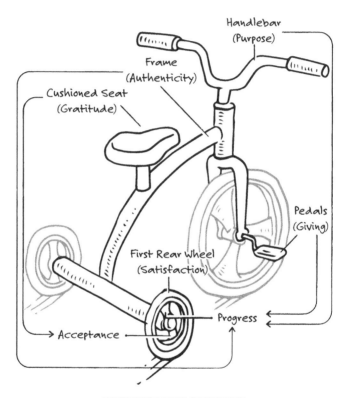

THE FIRST REAR WHEEL (SATISFACTION)

5. THE FIRST REAR WHEEL (SATISFACTION)

Satisfaction is the first rear supporting wheel of the tricycle. You achieve daily satisfaction by living an authentic life, practicing daily gratitude, leading a life of purpose, and giving. Two spokes support the satisfaction wheel— Acceptance and Progress.

A. THE FIRST SPOKE OF SATISFACTION WHEEL (ACCEPTANCE)

Acceptance is critical for satisfaction. Install it by practicing gratitude and treating life as almost perfect —a mix of sweet and sour.

B. THE SECOND SPOKE OF SATISFACTION WHEEL (PROGRESS)

Steady progress leads to satisfaction. Staying authentic, and living your purpose and commitment to giving, work together to speed up your progress.

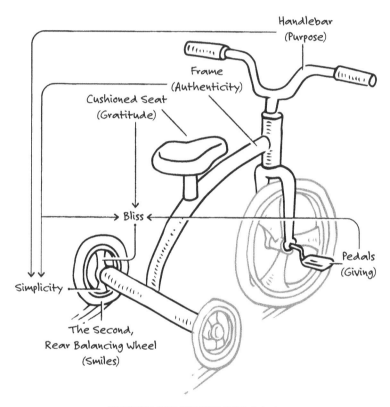

THE SECOND, REAR BALANCING WHEEL (SMILES)

6. THE SECOND, REAR BALANCING WHEEL (SMILES)

Smiles, the second rear supporting wheel of the tricycle, balances the satisfaction wheel. Both rear wheels need to move together, or the tricycle drags. Make a conscious effort to enjoy more smiles throughout the daily journey. More smiles appear as you live an authentic life of purpose, as a giver, practicing gratitude. Two spokes support the smiles wheel—Simplicity and Bliss.

A. THE FIRST SPOKE OF SMILES WHEEL (SIMPLICITY)

Achieve simplicity by practicing subtraction—decluttering your thoughts, tasks, and physical spaces. You simplify your life when you commit to living authentically—with purpose.

B. THE SECOND SPOKE OF SMILES WHEEL (BLISS)

Bliss arises from those moments you can create for yourself every day to nurture your soul. Staying authentic, practicing gratitude, and giving help in experiencing bliss. To enjoy regular doses of bliss, design them into your daily life. When you help others find their bliss, you fill your own life with it.

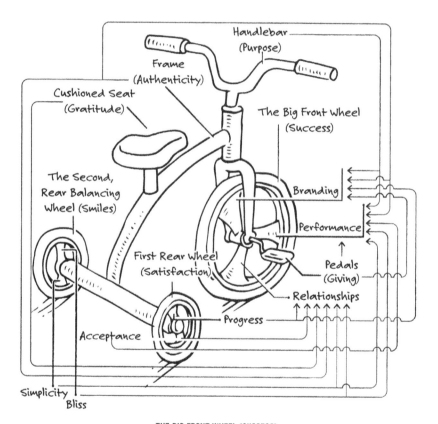

THE BIG FRONT WHEEL (SUCCESS)

7. THE BIG FRONT WHEEL (SUCCESS)

Success is the big front wheel of the tricycle. Focusing on daily satisfaction and more smiles will ensure broader, greater, sweeter-tasting success. Three spokes support this front wheel of Success—Relationships, Branding, and Performance.

A. THE FIRST SPOKE OF SUCCESS WHEEL (RELATIONSHIPS)

Good relationships make others want to see you flourish. They are motivated to help you and create opportunities for you. Authenticity and giving help develop a strong foundation for relationships. Gratitude enhances relationships. Acceptance and progress support relationship building. Simplicity and bliss help strengthen relationships.

B. THE SECOND SPOKE OF SUCCESS WHEEL (BRANDING)

Branding helps people discover and remember you for your unique abilities. It also helps instill trust and bring opportunities to you. For strong branding, be authentic and giving, find and go after your purpose, and focus on progress.

C. THE THIRD SPOKE OF SUCCESS WHEEL (PERFORMANCE)

Performance is the key to reinforcing trust in your abilities for new and repeat opportunities. Deliver higher performance by living an authentic life with purpose and giving. To achieve consistent performance, simplify, accept setbacks, and find bliss to keep your internal battery fully charged.

Do you see how the parts of the tricycle come together? How they interconnect and support each other? Do you notice how easy and intuitive it is to map your life to the tricycle we enjoyed as kids?

Learn about the unique strengths and design of your tricycle, as you assemble it. Adjust the parts for the most joyous ride without disrupting the basic safety of the design. Know what makes it unstable and how to repair its parts when needed, so it rides well at all times.

If you notice problems, don't compromise. Pull it apart and reassemble it. Focus on putting together your tricycle as suggested so that you can enjoy a fulfilling ride.

The fear of touching an unopened box may have been unnerving. But, trust me, the thrill of riding the first 100 feet on your newly assembled tricycle is priceless!

CHAPTER 10

THE MAINTENANCE

ONCE YOU GET used to the fun riding your tricycle, you won't want to stop. But pay close attention if you notice any issues, and fix it to prevent further damage.

For your car, you change the oil, rotate tires, replace brakes, and get an annual tune-up. Your tricycle also needs regular maintenance to navigate through life without breakdowns.

KEEP THE FRAME STRONG

The frame needs close monitoring and timely maintenance to prevent rust or bending. All the major parts are linked to it, and the tricycle depends on it. Check if and where you are inauthentic. Is it worth risking the relationships, reputation, and all that you've gained so far in life?

While going after success, there may be temptations to speak or act deceptively. It's easy to do since no one would know. Stay conscious of this trap and catch yourself before falling into it.

If you want continued success, satisfaction, and smiles—stay authentic.

REFILL SEAT CUSHION

Before riding your tricycle each day, make sure the seat cushion is thick with gratitude.

When things are going well, do you forget to be thankful? Do you take things for granted, puff up your ego, or ignore and mistreat people who support you?

Or, during rough times, do you switch into survival mode, letting fear and worry take over? Do you complain that life is unfair to you, and forget your blessings?

If so, you need to refill the seat cushion. If you already practice gratitude and keep a journal, add at least one new reason every day to be grateful.

ALIGN AND TIGHTEN THE HANDLEBAR

While riding my tricycle as a kid, sometimes the handlebar would loosen, get tilted, or come off, causing the tricycle to veer off the sidewalk onto the grass. At first, it was funny, but it quickly became awkward or painful.

When life throws curve balls at you, whether they are shiny opportunities or setbacks, it may steer you from the path, with no guarantee where you'll end up. That is the time to realign your life with a purpose to minimize the risk of getting lost. Your purpose will get you back on track toward satisfaction, with lots of smiles, and as you enjoy continued success.

ALIGN AND TIGHTEN PEDALS

When you are a giver, your friends, relatives, and well-wishers may tell you to stop being naïve — that others may be taking advantage of you. Time to let them know that it's not possible to con a giver because the act of giving is voluntary. No one can force you to give. Don't lose faith in giving — that's how you move all the wheels forward and receive from the universe as well as from those you helped.

In good times when you're feeling super lucky, don't stop giving. Don't let success make you think that the world should report to you, and that you've given enough. Remind yourself that what you have received is a result of having given to others. Especially don't stop giving during tough times.

Continue to find new ways to give and have like-minded givers as your friends. There's always enough to give, even if not in material form. Keep giving — it is the only thing you can do.

FIX ANY PROBLEMS WITH WHEELS AND SPOKES

For a tricycle to move ahead, each wheel should rotate with minimal friction and at the same speed. Smiles and Satisfaction should move in sync with Success for a pleasant journey through life.

Acceptance and Progress are the Spokes for Satisfaction. Simplicity and Bliss are the Spokes for Smiles. Relationships, Branding, and Performance are the Spokes for Success.

You already know how the individual spokes provide strength to the wheels. Check the integrity of the spokes and repair issues that crop up. That will ensure that the wheels are always sturdy and spin in sync, pushing your tricycle along its path.

TAKE CARE OF YOUR TIRES

Tires represent physical and mental health. Neglecting them will sap your energy and lead your tricycle to wobble as if it has a flat tire. You may even stall.

Proper diet, exercise, and sleep will keep these tires inflated so you can enjoy the ride without skidding or dragging. When your body is prepared to support your mind wherever it wants to go, you enjoy the ride.

When I was in the race, chasing success, I talked myself out of physical exercise. To make things worse, I found comfort in junk food, using it as an anti-anxiety drug. Eventually, I fell ill.

My blood test showed sugar levels three times higher than normal and fat levels more than eight times normal. Additional tests revealed a 90 percent blockage in the main arteries that supply blood to my heart—a critical condition which could lead to a heart attack. It could have happened anytime, but I was unaware till the doctor broke the news. My family was in a state of shock and acute worry. I was scared too, since other lives depend on me—and it wasn't their fault.

After multiple surgical procedures and many days in intensive care at the hospital, I came home with a box full of medicines—prescribed for the foreseeable future. The doctor said I needed a lifestyle change to stay alive. As a nutritionist and health coach, my wife helped me change my diet, add exercise, and sleep better for a lifestyle with vitality and vigor.

I invited this potentially fatal heart condition by allowing so much internal damage to build up. I wouldn't have lived to publish this book if I hadn't made those changes. I'm on the right track now. I work out seven days a week and try to follow a healthy diet even as I travel globally. These allow me to work on keeping the tires of my tricycle in top shape — with positivity and strength.

CLEAN YOUR TRICYCLE OF NEGATIVITY BUILDUP

As you ride your tricycle, dirt and grime may collect on it. If not cleaned, they lead to drag, even bringing your tricycle to a complete halt. Dirt and grime represent Greed, Resentment, Jealousy, and Vanity, which you must clean as part of maintenance.

A. GREED

Greed is an obsession to get money and fame beyond what's needed for a comfortable life. This behavior stems from low self-esteem. It grows out of a notion that you are the way others see you. In its worst form, greed becomes an obsession that is satisfied at the cost of others, perhaps even illegally.

Keep checking if greed is driving you to dishonesty or immoral acts. Do you need more than what you already have? Why are you pushing so hard to get it? What are you risking in this endless chase? Staying authentic and driven by purpose can keep your greed in check.

B. **RESENTMENT**

At times you may feel judged, wronged, or a victim of unfair treatment. You may react with bitterness toward offenders, employers, customers, even society in general. The longer you carry resentment in your heart, the deeper it digs in and the more it disturbs you. It distorts the lens you use to look at people and life in general. It can even push you to hurt others or yourself.

Look within to see if you're carrying such baggage. For relief, express your feelings and talk about them with someone you trust to give you another perspective. If you can't find a logical explanation for what happened, let acceptance help reduce resentment.

C. **JEALOUSY**

Jealousy stems from comparisons that make you feel unwanted, not good enough, or like you're losing a race. It builds a negative attitude toward those you compare yourself to. You feel it in the form of fear, concern, or unease —which makes you distrusting, suspicious, and critical.

If you live an authentic life, driven by purpose and the intention of giving, it's less likely to happen. But if you do catch yourself feeling jealous, reminding yourself of what you already have will wipe away the grime.

D. **VANITY**

Do you brag about your background, wins, or net worth? Do you think you're better than others or know more than they do? Watch for that fine line between being confident and being cocky. While you may feel that you are on top of the world, you risk coming across to others as an arrogant jerk.

Like jealousy, carrying an inflated self-image stems from personal insecurities and the need to validate your status in the eyes of others. You were born with your background—no extra credit if you lucked out. And your successes resulted in part from the contributions of many others. So why are you bragging?

If you stay authentic you don't claim undue credit. Remember your purpose and see successes only as milestones. Feel and express gratitude for all those who helped you along the way. This approach will keep vanity in check.

THE DAILY QUESTION

YOU'VE LEARNED EVERYTHING there is to know about *The Tricycle Way* that allowed me to transform my life. Think through the Frame, Cushioned Seat, Handlebar, Pedals, Wheels, Spokes, and Tires. Assemble your tricycle, then stay on top of the upkeep. Don't let your life come to a standstill.

Check up on your tricycle at the beginning and end of each day. Get into the practice of asking yourself twice daily: *How's my tricycle?* In the morning, the answer will reveal what needs attention—and you already know how to deal with it. Toward the end of the day, ask the question again to see how far you got and if any additional issues surfaced. You may be quick in diagnosing problems, but fixes may take time. That's OK—it's a journey. My own story is living proof that *The Tricycle Way* works. Convinced? Jump on and make it yours.

EPILOGUE

THIS BOOK IS for the person you see in the mirror every day
—and that's you. And here's my claim: If you go *The Tricycle
Way* and start focusing first on daily satisfaction and more
smiles, it will lead to broader, greater, sweeter-tasting success.
You'll stop racing through life and start enjoying the ride.

Even if you're not a success maniac, it will help you lead
a balanced life with peace, freedom, fortune, and fun only few
can imagine.

Your tricycle as it is today defines who you are, how you
think, and the journey of life you're experiencing. If you already enjoy daily satisfaction and are all smiles and successful
—kudos, more power to you. Otherwise, consider this book
as a guide to make the needed changes.

Everything you learned in this book is easy to understand.
Based on my journey, I know it works. The fact you've read
this book is a sign that you want to bring changes to your life
for reaching your ideal prospect.

Do you see a part of you in the characters of Jim and Sue? Heather helped them understand what was wrong, why, and how to fix it. You have this book.

Discovering and rebuilding my tricycle has been an exciting and transformative journey. And it isn't over yet. Every day offers a chance for me to learn and experience new ways to ride around and enjoy it. I'm getting to know my tricycle better. I understand the way it works, when it has issues, and what it takes to fix it.

While riding it, I don't think about its parts. But when I face a situation or challenge, the tricycle pops into my head, highlighting the part that needs attention.

At a party, a friend offered me a partnership in a new, lucrative business venture. The tricycle flashed with a skewed handlebar, indicating misalignment with my purpose. I declined.

At another social event, I witnessed an ego match among a few successful entrepreneurs — who works the hardest, sleeps the least, takes the most medication, and travels the most. It reminded me of my past when I won such contests. For a moment a voice deep inside me said: *hey, you've got to get ahead and get back in the game.* But I squished that bug since I saw the tricycle with deflated tires, reminding me to take care of my health.

My children now want to spend time with me and share their challenges and wins. My wife has started throwing surprise birthday parties for me again. She still yells at me and sends me to the doghouse, but I'm out sooner now.

I'm not perfect by any standards. But I've become better

at knowing who I am and where I'm going, what's wrong with me, and how to fix it.

I've been fine-tuning my tricycle since I assembled it. It helps when you know your patterns and what to do when you have issues. I'm the creator, the mechanic, and the rider of my tricycle, and it still pays to ask myself every day: *how's my tricycle?*

Take the time, with the right mindset as the tool, to assemble your tricycle. It will bring a sense of joy, control, fulfillment, and wins beyond what I can express. You must experience it first-hand by going through the process.

This book is my gift to you. I hope it will make you think, challenge your habits, and give you a different point of view for building the life that you'd love to live every day. Go ahead! Assemble your tricycle and start enjoying the ride.

ABOUT THE AUTHOR

Born in India—raised by a father who was a fountain of wisdom and the most caring mother—Sanjog had a wonderful childhood. But, just before his college graduation, he lost his father to a heart attack. Overnight, his secure and comfortable life vanished, and the loss forced him to mature. Soon he decided that sheer survival wouldn't be enough and developed a burning need to become big.

To accelerate his growth, he immigrated to the United States as a software programmer. Soon, he realized that a regular 9–5 job didn't bring out the best in him. So he started his own business.

Initially, growing his business became an obsession and even getting married or having children didn't slow him down. But, before it was too late, he realized his mistakes and transformed from a success maniac to a happy rider going *The Tricycle Way.*

Today, Sanjog is an entrepreneur, coach, strategic consultant, and a professional moderator specializing in enterprise IT. He has independently fashioned himself into a subject matter expert and thought leader for the C-suite audience through the institutions he has built: CIO Talk Network (CTN), the IT consulting firm AVVAL, and Real-IT-y, a community give-back program.

CTN is an IT media company with an audience in over 110 countries. It features thought leadership contributed by global enterprise business and IT practitioners, industry analysts, and subject matter experts through podcasts, blogs, and executive events. As the founder and show host of CTN, Sanjog has interviewed over 1,000 C-suite IT executives from global enterprises including the New York Stock Exchange, MasterCard, NASA, the Department of Defense, and the United Nations. To learn more, visit www.CIOTalkNetwork.com.

AVVAL, with U.S. clients ranging from venture-backed startups to Fortune 500 firms, helps companies manage their IT workforce through staffing, talent management, and leadership development services. As CEO of AVVAL, Sanjog helps organizations solve their IT talent and leadership issues. As a coach, using *The Tricycle Way* framework, he grooms IT leaders and professionals to become better individuals and performers. To learn more, visit www.AVVAL.com.

Real-IT-y helps mesh classroom learning with practical business insights through workshops using roleplays inspired by real IT scenarios. Sanjog facilitates these workshops with support from local IT leaders as volunteers.

Sanjog strives to remain a neutral voice with a trustworthy tone, and his work helps not only to cultivate current leaders but to build future ones. For his accomplishments and contributions, Sanjog was selected as one of the *Top 100 under 50 Diverse Executive Leaders for 2013* by Diversity MBA Magazine.

Sanjog lives a fulfilling and joyous life in Chicago with his wife and two children. Visit him at www.SanjogAul.com.

NOTES

NOTES

NOTES

NOTES

NOTES

NOTES

NOTES

NOTES

NOTES